KISSING THE WAVES

BEYOND THE VALE PAPERBACK

© Copyright 2023
Valentia Smith Kadalie

The right of Valentia Smith Kadalie to be identified as the author of this work has been asserted by her in accordance with the Copyright, Designs and Patents Act 1988.

All Rights Reserved

Any redistribution or reproduction of part or all of the content in any form is prohibited other than the following: a reviewer who might quote brief passages in a review.

The author does not grant you any other rights in relation to the material and content of this publication.

You may not adapt, edit, change, transform, publish, republish, distribute, redistribute, broadcast or rebroadcast in public the material contained in this publication without the author's written consent.

ISBN 978-0-6397-6109-1

First Published in 2023

Beyond The Vale Publishing
www.beyondthevalepublishing.com

Cover picture painted by Patti Fish – PraiseArt
Title inspired by Werner Momberg – Mergon Foundation

Valentia Smith Kadalie

KISSING THE WAVES

Contents

Introduction 7
Dedication and Acknowledgements 9
Val's Foreword 12
Editor's Comments 13
Endorsments 21
Chapter One 31
Chapter Two 57
Chapter Three 63
Chapter Four 67
Chapter Five 76
Chapter Six 86
Chapter Seven 101
Chapter Eight 115
Chapter Nine 130
Chapter Ten 145
Chapter Eleven 155
Chapter Twelve 169
Chapter Thirteen 182
Chapter Fourteen 193
Chapter Fifteen 201

Introduction

I have learned to kiss the wave that struck me against the Rock of Ages - C. H. Spurgeon (1834 - 1892)

This narrative must begin with the immortal wisdom of Rudyard Kipling. Of course, he is forgiven for not including the female gender in his epic poem – he was not only a path-dependent man but a product of encultured chauvinism. He described himself as "a God-fearing Christian atheist."[1] He certainly had a way with words!

I have seen and experienced miracles of my God's intervention in my life and the lives of others. My narrative will feature the tapestry woven by my God's Master Hand in weaving the story that is part of my journey through life.

The buffeting, merciless waves of many tsunamis led me to understand what my God wanted to teach me. My more focused discipleship ministry began to evolve.

---

1 Derbyshire, J (2006). National Review. https://www.nationalreview.com/corner/kiplings-religion-john-derbyshire/

IF

If you can keep your head when all about you
Are losing theirs and blaming it on you,
If you can trust yourself when all men doubt you,
But make allowance for their doubting too.
If you can wait and not be tired by waiting,
Or being lied about, don't deal in lies,
Or being hated, don't give way to hating,
And yet don't look too good, nor talk too wise:
If you can dream—and not make dreams your master.
If you can think—and not make thoughts your aim.
If you can meet with Triumph and Disaster
And treat those two impostors just the same.
If you can bear to hear the truth you've spoken
Twisted by knaves to make a trap for fools,
Or watch the things you gave your life to, broken,
And stoop and build 'em up with worn-out tools:
If you can make one heap of all your winnings
And risk it on one turn of pitch-and-toss,
And lose, and start again at your beginnings
And never breathe a word about your loss;
If you can force your heart and nerve and sinew
To serve your turn long after they are gone,
And so hold on when there is nothing in you
Except for the will which says to them: 'Hold on!'
If you can talk with crowds and keep your virtue,
Or walk with Kings—nor lose the common touch,
If neither foes nor loving friends can hurt you,
If all men count with you, but none too much;
If you can fill the unforgiving minute
With sixty seconds' worth of distance run,
Yours is the Earth and everything that's in it,
And—which is more—you'll be a Man, my son!

Dedication and Acknowledgements

I dedicate this book to Stanley and Thelma, my parents. I think of them now as on countless other days! Daddy, you were one of a kind. I am sure you are having hilarious conversations with God and everyone in Heaven about how things should have been done. The discussion on a recent radio show about the medicinal uses of cannabis reminded me of you punting this fact five decades ago.

Mommy, as you rest in your heavenly mansion, remember that your unconditional mother's love has shaped my life. I continue to quote your Thelmarisms, and I hope you are not cracking plates on any heads. I hope that dad has not had cause to punch a hole through your bedroom wall to watch TV!

To my husband Charles, who could see angels when I was too distressed to see them and to whom I owe my life and our discipling ministry. Our lives together were settled in the eternal plans of our gracious Lord. Charles, you are the epitome of understanding and the love that will not let me go. You are a dad who set an example of fatherhood to our children.

To our children, Robyn, Lisa and Rico, you have enriched my life with joy and laughter while teaching me about being a family. As we say in Afrikaans, "niemand kan vir julle klaarmaak[2]".

To my grandchildren in the USA, Jade, Kyla, Halle, Hunter and Izzy, you have made me the happiest of internet grandmothers. Your sparkle, energy, and smiling faces remind me of the joyous days of my childhood.

To my siblings Carol, William, Patti, Ricky and Vivie, I am always blessed and encouraged when we share childhood memories that make us laugh. We remain a strong and loyal family unit.

To my beloved friends Rina, Alida and Luthando – in Heaven. 14 September 2015 marked the most tragic event in my life. As I daily remember your life lived for Him, I have learned "not to feel overcome with grief to the point of losing sight of the truth". I have learned to cling to the truth of God's Word. The birds and the flowers of the seasons remind me daily of those truths. I have learned to lay my grief at His feet. I know we shall meet in Heaven.

To the precious heroes of transformation, some of whom are mentioned in this book, from whom I have learned so much – you are the grains of salt our country desperately needs. Our Lord Jesus reached out to you, and in turn, you opened your arms to others as you discipled those for whom He died.

To the mentors and role models mentioned in this book that have shaped my life and ministry, thank you for the building blocks you offered me. No other foundation would have stood

---

2 Nobody can do better than you.

the test of the numerous destructive tsunamis that intruded into my life were it not for you and what you shared.

To my editor, who asked me to write my story - you asked for it, and I sent you reams of notes, scattered thoughts and script! The incalculable days and hours working on my draft and our many chats have resulted in this bound record. By the way, Charles and I wonder about God's purpose in using you to assist in my written odyssey. Our friendship remains, and we continue to contribute to each other's journey in ways that show my God's planning. Thank you for proofreading and editing this book – pro bono.

My story is a chronicle of those who impacted and shared my life; thank you for being part of my journey.

Valentia Smith Kadalie.

Val's Foreword

Disturb us, Lord, when
We are too well pleased with ourselves,
When our dreams have come true
Because we have dreamed too little,
When we arrived safely
Because we sailed too close to the shore.
Disturb us, Lord, when
With the abundance of things we possess
We have lost our thirst
For the waters of life;
Having fallen in love with life,
We have ceased to dream of eternity
And in our efforts to build a new earth,
We have allowed our vision
Of the new Heaven to dim.
Disturb us, Lord, to dare more boldly,
To venture on wider seas
Where storms will show your mastery;
Where losing sight of land,
We shall find the stars.
We ask You to push back
The horizons of our hopes;
And to push into the future
In strength, courage, hope, and love.

        Author Unknown

Editor's Comments

Arguably, the growing threats of the 21st century cause many to wonder about the place, relevance and witness of divided Christian denominations – known individually as a Church[3]. For instance, the apologetics offered by competing and divided denominations purporting to read the same Bible, pray to and worship the same God – but never under the same roof as those with a different tradition - is confusing and dilutes trust in a body of people[4] who offer a product (salvation) and service (care and compassion) under brands with stringent entry conditions.

Cynics wonder why Christian missionaries cross oceans and borders with the Gospel but neglect their neighbours when on home assignment. Why do many leaders and others in their denomination spend more time at conferences, drinking tea and beer with colleagues but seldom (if ever) sit or walk alongside those likened to "sheep without a shepherd[5]"? How

---

3 The word "church" derives from the Greek – εκκλησία. Church, originally meant an assembly called out by the magistrate, or by legitimate authority. It was in this last sense that the word was adapted and applied by the writers of the New Testament to the Christian congregation. So, the church now meets in buildings. The believers of those called out by God – the called-out ones, the elect chosen before the foundation of the world (Ephesians 1.4).
4 Matthew 12.25 and Mark 3.25.
5 Matthew 9.36.

can Christians say they believe the Bible is God's Word but do not share its divine message with those nearest them?

> And even if our gospel is veiled, it is veiled to those who are perishing. The god of this age has blinded the minds of unbelievers so that they cannot see the light of the gospel that displays the glory of Christ, who is the image of God[6].

Arguably, then, the strong words of Jesus to the Pharisees[7] can also apply to Christians – many of whom are part of a denomination.

So what has gone wrong? The endemic tsunamis of sectarianism and human nature clog denominations. Petty rules, archaic traditions, self-perpetuating hierarchies, happy clappy concerts, and an overabundance of gossip (often framed in prayers) keep churchgoers captive. Fashion shows regularly entertain and dilute the core purpose of the church[8].

In contrast, Valentia Kadalie draws attention to the vision of Christ and his mission for the church. This objective is the privileged responsibility of every believer. Val shows how Christian discipleship – the task of Christians - builds redemptive bridges across barriers. Val takes readers to the road less travelled by Churchianity – accountable discipleship[9].

However, and non-judgmentally, Val points out that Christians are human beings – in whatever denomination. Marred by internal and external forces[10], Christians are imperfect.

---

6 2 Corinthians 4. 3-5.
7 Matthew 23. 1-12.
8 Matthew 28. 18-20.
9 Matthew 28. 18-20.
10 Jeremiah 18. 1-12.

One beggar tells and shows other beggars where to find food[11].

A redeeming relationship with the Lord Jesus Christ does not ipso facto create a new personality. An intellectual signing on the bottom line does not sponge away the innate formative years of a damaged childhood and harsh adult experiences. Heritage, social, political, and economic factors indiscriminately influence young and old. Consequently, Val advocates for victorious spiritual growth (sanctification). Following The Jesus of the Cross is the underlying byproduct of Christian discipleship. Val invites readers to join others sitting at her accountability kitchen table. Crucially, Val emphasises that Jesus expresses His love for His church. So, against an otherwise bleak generalization of the impotent, divisive and chaotic church scenario, readers will be challenged by her timely 21st-Century wake-up story about the church's mission in a chaotic South African Rainbow Nation.

Val's narrative includes information about herself, her family, her friends, her God – and Christian discipleship. A spiritual conversion to accept Christ as Saviour is the doorway to living out the Gospel and then discipling others to enjoy their relationship with the Lord Jesus Christ and simultaneously grow in grace and the love of Christ.

Val Kadalie's literary odyssey will touch each reader's heart and mind. She shares her freshly invigorated Damascus Road experience[12] - her pilgrimage of faith. Val shares the highs and lows of her mind-boggling journey with candour and humour,

---
[11] Adapted from Miles, D. T. cited in https://www.canadianlutheran.ca/beggars-telling-beggars-where-to-find-food/
[12] The religious conversion of Saul of Tarsus to Paul the Apostle of Christ (Acts 9: 1-9; Acts 22: 6 -11 and Acts 26: 9 – 10).

enriched by her thematic metaphor-laced focus on numerous destructive tsunamis. We will get to know Charles, her devoted and supportive husband - "the rock-solid anchor" who introduced her to what she describes as "their ministry". Despite his bouts of ill health, Charles stood alongside Val as she courageously challenged political, commercial and social injustices. He enabled her to survive a catalogue of medical emergencies and intense personal suffering while mourning the deaths of close friends.

Readers will trace Val's formative family years as a developing child, teenager and adult in Cape Town at the southern tip of Apartheid-divided South Africa. We will be introduced to her parents, children, organisations and the people who played and still play memorable roles in her life. One example is the founder of the Cape Town City Mission - formerly the City Slum Mission. The missionary work of F. G. Lowe exemplified the spiritual paradigm that inspired Val's faith journey. Walking in the footsteps of Lowe and others of faith now influences her relationships with people in the newly billed Apartheid-free Rainbow Nation.

Val resurrects concerns about the infamy of incompetent governance, endemic corruption in high places, misplaced nationalism and the problems caused by the self-serving, personalised structuring of many Christian denominations. Accordingly, Val points to the Pharisees' practices, which had earned the biting condemnation of Jesus[13]. Consequently, as committed Christians, Val and Charles have deconstructed a common understanding of the Church. Their initiative might offend some readers, but others might argue that they have a

---

[13] Matthew 23. 13-36.

point – backed by the Bible. So, why not read on and assess their evidence? Readers will find the philosophy of Charles and Val thought-provoking, illuminating, and liberating. They serve us food for thought about what it is to be the earth's salt and the world's light. They point us to the pioneer disciples of Christ who, according to the Bible, turned their Romanised world upside down – as disciples[14].

Core to Val's journey is her empathy for the aged. Alongside is her ministry to psychologically shattered individuals ostracized by society and often the Church. Val's Christ-focused ministry personifies the words of Jesus, "a bruised reed he shall not break and a smoking flax he will not quench[15]. Readers can learn much from each of her specific experiences. One example is how she and Charles learned empathy as voluntary patients in a hospital for those suffering from mental illnesses.

The evidence in this narrative shows that their relationship with God has infused them with fresh spiritual vigour, freedom and growth as children of God's Kingdom. They have embraced the church's mission to teach others about God's redemption, actively disciple them and point the way for them to grow in grace and the love of Christ.

Val and Charles are among the many believers in Jesus globally who have returned to the core Christian ministry of discipleship. Some people may resign from a denomination or seek to revive staid, ineffective, stuck-in-the-mud Christian bodies. Still, these two disciples of Christ do not compete with or seek to change any traditional representation of the Church.

---

14 Acts 17.6.
15 The need to disciple people as in the ministry of Jesus who reached out to the spiritually, physically, or morally weak. A bruised reed is damaged, but not irreparable. A "smouldering wick" may soon be snuffed out, but it can glow again (Matthew 12.20).

They are not trying to rearrange the chairs on the Titanic. Their focus is Christian discipleship. They do not pander to the greed of the prosperity cults. They do not concern themselves with the private-jet-served religious leaders. They remain unphased by the populist revivalist fly-by-night groups and the grandiose glitter of some mega-churches (indeed, all that glitters is not gold – but fool's gold). They do not contribute to head-counting competitiveness, arguing about baptism, and debating the Second Coming of Jesus. They have no ego-centric need to micro-manage believers; tell them what clothes they must wear and how and where they should spend their recreational time. They focus on making disciples, not building a shaky and irrelevant "holier-than-others" brand. Arguably, their lives and ministry show there is more to being a child of God than paying homage to archaic rituals' peripheral practices. Val and Charles understand the many dimensions of Christian discipleship. They have shared the concept in this down-to-earth narrative.

The final chapter highlights other tsunamis and various topical realities. The reader will gain a deeper insight into Val's incisive scalpel-like mindset where her humanity, ethics and logic challenge injustice, incompetence, and caring compassion born out of her empathy. Her candid story gives readers an insight into her down-to-earth focus on the need for Christian discipleship to awaken and challenge familiar yet unmet sociopolitical and economic challenges. After all, "faith without works is dead[16]", and, arguably, "Churchianity" is a heretical violation of and a sham substitute for the Gospel[17] message. Churchianity replicates the scenario that caused Jesus to

---

16 James 2. 14-26.
17 Jude 1.3.

castigate the Pharisees[18]. Christian discipleship calls out Churchianity because its destructive climate has changed "the faith once delivered to the saints[19]". Arguably, the time is now, and restoring discipleship is imperative – a core part of the way forward.

Val's mini-autobiography ultimately hones in on the ministry she and Charles have adopted. Her riveting pen pictures invite personal reflection. Similarly, her unassailable integrity, evidence-driven determination, unwavering focus, transparent humanity, and sincere and committed faith calls for the supportive prayers of Christians.

Val's appeal to the Bible, her unconditional compassion, and references to appropriate snippets of history, politics, the fumbling 21st-Century Church, and COVID-19 bolster her balanced emotional and rational argument for every believer to return to Christian discipleship.

Val's pen pictures address specific incidents (topics) that do not always follow a chronological sequence of events. Consequently, her collation of facts enables readers to focus on the pulse of her written experiences. Her frequent use of "my" helps readers concentrate on her mini-autobiography – for which she is accountable. The content comes from the pen of an experienced and enthusiastic believer who warts and all rejoices in Christ's redeeming work.

So, welcome to Val's personal battles against the Apartheid tsunami, in tandem with the other tsunamis that came her way. Her focus on discipleship will invoke reactions, and rest

---

18 Matthew 18.
19 Jude 1-4.

assured she will field every response – her large kitchen table awaits.

Why not contact Val and Charles by email? They can be reached at: val@ontheedgesa.org.za

Endorsements

Endorsement 1

"Kissing the Waves" is a beautiful tapestry of insightful observations and life lessons learned through a wide array of unforgettable experiences in the long and winding journey of Charles and Val Kadalie.

As you work through her story, you will find that *On the Edge* is not just the name of the ministry that Val and Charles started. It is how they have lived their lives! Val will take you to the edge of a divided nation in these pages: systemic injustice, broken people, death, despair, and defeat. But the beauty of what she has written is that she won't leave you on the ragged edge or allow you to plunge over the cliff into darkness. She will get you to the other side of the issues where there is restoration, peace, laughter, and hope.

Val's life journey's vignettes speak of incredible character forged in the fire of adversity. Through constant trauma and challenge, she has proven the spiritual principle that light drives out the darkness. Through tireless effort, she has seen that same light multiply in and through others.

I have known Charles and Val for a very long time, and I count it as one of the great privileges of my life to call them friends. I have observed their journey, learned from their actions, and admired their impact. My life is richer because I walked with Charles and Val Kadalie. Your life will be richer when you read her book, so turn the page and start learning to kiss the waves!

Harry Brown
President
New Generations

Endorsement 2

There are few people like Charles and Val Kadalie whose lives define the words of Jesus in John 10:10, "I have come that you may have life, and life in all its [fullness] abundance".

In "Kissing The Waves", readers will come across numerous events in the life of Val Kadalie. This extraordinary narrative is about a profoundly ordinary woman and her amazing husband and family who defied darkness's forces. She challenged the enforced submission to Apartheid, bureaucratic bungling and gloomy pessimism.

Her story is about her family, who redefined what is generally described as traditional family life. Her ministry shows how by discipling the lives of others, we receive new concepts of community and country. Val Kadalie was not born to settle down and mind her own business. Her youthful encounter with God filled her with the courage to defy mediocrity.

Born in an era of race, class, economic oppression, unrest and revolution, she poignantly reflects on how living as a Christian and citizen influenced her life and her perspectives. So many of us today do not have any courage to speak up and out. Val Kadalie has made it her life's work to speak up and out and follow up by doing – because doing is what defines her. In "Kissing the Waves", she records countless occasions when she stood alone, believed alone, and acted alone with her husband Charles, children and God as her only allies.

Her story is borne out of courageous convictions and life-changing encounters. She demonstrates that believing in the power of those still-quiet thoughts of multiple revolutions is necessary. Fuelled by ideas, "things don't have to be like this," she went out to fix the things that "did not have to be like this." For example, she focuses on restoring Christian discipleship to its rightful place in society.

Val Kadalie's story is about an everyday retired professional woman whose encounters with God gave her the courage to kiss the tsunami waves. These waves often smashed into her, but she discovered hope and healing in the Rock of Ages. God shaped her and did not allow her to be destroyed. Her experiences and faith are lessons a broken country and troubled people must learn from urgently.

Lorenzo A Davids
Chief Executive Officer
The Justice Fund

Endorsement 3

"Kissing the Waves" is a book that will change attitudes, kill misperceptions and destroy preconceived ideas. Be prepared to unconditionally open your heart and mind and absorb life experiences from the pen of a woman who has made it her aim to be effective. Ask the Lord to remove all fear and threat to whatever you stand for. Then you will be able to reap value from the narrative.

I recall the day at the kitchen table ... two more distinctly removed individuals I could not imagine. The White Afrikaner (me) – the epitome of Apartheid, and the Other Coloured – the fighter for righteousness and justice (Val).

God-given grace and insight balance Val Kadalie's outlook and practice - a sense of justice and fairness for all, irrespective of colour, creed or financial status. Val and Charles have succeeded in weaving the Gospel of Jesus and disciple-making into the 20th century and beyond. Still, there are more stories to tell.

Growing up in the Apartheid era and being discriminated against, Val has perfected the art of juggling. A harsh discriminatory environment, on the one hand, and the ability in her capacity as an individual, leader, mother and Jesus disciple to balance God's vision of God's grace against all odds.

Extremely evident is how she defines onslaughts on her physical and spiritual being as the tsunamis. The golden thread is how Val, with God's assistance, has (thus far) overcome these onslaughts throughout her seventy-plus years of life.

Val belongs to a unique body of Christ:

> The general assembly and church of the firstborn who are registered in heaven; to God, the Judge of all, to the spirits of just men made perfect, to Jesus the Mediator of the new covenant ... [20]

Mariette Maartens
Chairperson
Cape Town City Mission

---

[20] Hebrews 12:23

Endorsement 4

Charles and Val Kadalie's lives and ministry have significantly impacted my wife and me.

Their ministry, *On The Edge,* is the most transformational ministry that I have ever experienced.

Val's book will help you understand why they've made this kind of impact on those they've worked with.

You will laugh, cry, be disturbed, and be challenged to make disciples as Jesus did.

Brad Sprague
Coaching leaders and teams in making disciples
Novo and Twofoureight

Endorsement 5

From the first meeting, I knew that Charles and Val Kadalie were some of the most incredible people I would ever meet. They embraced my family and opened the doors for me to learn about Disciple Making Movements. Soon, Val had become my "Cape Town Mom", and I would visit whenever I was in the city.

I cannot think of anyone more qualified than her to write on this topic. Her life is a testimony of faith and endurance against incredible odds. I have watched her overcome some of the challenges described in this book. She faces each obstacle with amazing grace, resolve and determination.

Val and I grew up in the same country but in entirely different worlds. Our country's painful past affected her in ways I can only understand by listening to the stories. Every time we talk, I appreciate her world and life even more. She never ceases to astound me with her humility and dedication to the gospel, no matter how difficult things get. Many people talk about following Jesus and making disciples. Val Kadalie lives it every minute of every day.

This book details the life of an extraordinary journey with Jesus. Her best book has already been written in the lives of her disciples. I have read those books written into the lives of those she has impacted. They have enthralled and amazed me. This book explains why her life has made such an extraordinary impact. I pray that you relish her story with the joy and delight it brought me.

David Broodryk
Executive Director
Twofoureight

Chapter One

Me, the waves of the Apartheid tsunami, Stanley Smith, Thelma, and domesticity

I must introduce you to the formative events that led me to be who I am, my life, career choices, and my faith-built focus on my God. These factors enabled me to surf the waves of Apartheid's tsunami and those of other tsunamis.

My focus

> For we are God's handiwork, created in Christ Jesus to do good works, which God prepared in advance for us to do[21]

The Apartheid tsunami

Growing up the eldest of six siblings, I did not know about Ephesians Chapter 2. I would not have appreciated or understood its truth. I also had little grasp of the legally constructed Apartheid tsunami that flooded our streets and destroyed homes. Commerce, industry, defence, police forces and our courts worshipped at its shrine. Apartheid created barriers – and impacted my family. I would not have

---

21 Ephesians 2.10.

comprehended how prayerful exegetes of the Christian religion[22] could guarantee the support of Divine authority[23] for their religious-politically concocted Apartheid tsunami that swept aside justice, peace and goodwill to all.

This is the story of my God's grace, mercy, power and gift of faith. He enabled me to kiss the waves of the Apartheid tsunami (and others), endure and triumph over the cudgels of ill health, snuggle into the warm embraces of my husband Charles, and live abundantly under the cloak of my redeeming Saviour, the Lord Jesus Christ. Consequently, I am part of that company of people ministering to others.

As it was in the beginning

When my parents were in the second trimester of pregnancy with me, on 18 June 1951, South African President Dr D. F. Malan announced the Separate Representation of Voters Bill. I did not know that we designated coloured people were no longer allowed to vote in the Cape. I was unaware that Black South Africans suffered a similar fate fifteen years earlier, in 1936. Apartheid's evil talons were officially and legally bared to impact South Africa's most precious heritage. Its First People and those whose skin was not white bore the brunt of the Apartheid ideology. Its evil carried the influences of the uninvited arrival of settlers of Dutch and English culture.

The Population Registration Act No 30 of 1950 was passed on 7 July 1950. This law required people to be identified and

---

22 Romans 13. This verse served also to affirm the so-called Divine Right of Kings (Britannica https://www.britannica.com/topic/divine-right-of-kings).

23 Many politically biased theologians have often justified apartheid and slavery by appealing to the so-called curse of Ham (Genesis 9: 22-29) where designated peoples were to be "hewers of wood and drawers of water (servants) forever.

registered as White, Coloured, Bantu (Black African) or Other. I was born one year later and registered as "Other Coloured".

In May 1951 (the year I was born), The War Veterans Torch Commandos, consisting of White veterans opposing the government, led mass protests against the Separate Representation of Voters Bill – they were not successful in removing the statute. The Franchise Action Council launched a rally in Cape Town. Most schools closed for a day, protesting the controversial Voters Bill. In December 1951, Nelson "Madiba" Mandela was banned under the Riotous Assemblies Act and later imprisoned on Robben Island. He ultimately triumphed in his goal of bringing democracy to South Africa. He became the first democratically elected president in 1994 – citizenship and the right to vote were the right of all South Africans.

I am sure those were worrying times to parent a new baby. Moreso, five more children were born to my parents over the next fifteen years. The Apartheid tsunami waves caused heartaches and fuelled repressed anger. Apartheid's unjust, arbitrary, discriminatory nature was epitomised by Steve Biko, an activist murdered by the South African security police on 12 September 1977.

> Apartheid, both petty and grand, is obviously evil. Nothing can justify the arrogant assumption that a clique of foreigners has the right to decide on the lives of the majority.
>
> Steve Biko (1946 – 1977)

The emerging struggle against the Apartheid tsunami

There were many tough and violence-driven years when the Apartheid tsunami swept across the southern tip of Africa. Like a whirlpool, the legislated decrees inexorably sucked people into a politically encased abyss that denied them the franchise and human right to freedom of association. Consequently, open and clandestine political struggles gestated and emerged.

A protest march, a massacre and Bantustans

The Sharpeville massacre blighted our history on 21 March 1960. Armed police fired on a defenceless crowd of anti-pass law protesters at the Sharpeville police station. They killed sixty-nine people and wounded 186. On the same day, 1400 km away, anti-pass demonstrators in Langa near Cape Town were shot at by police leaving two dead and twenty-nine injured. Nine days later, on 30 March 1960, hiding behind my father at our front door, I watched (in fascination but with no understanding) an army of men marching on Settler's Way. On that day, police violently assaulted inhabitants of Langa, targeting "migrant" workers. Almost spontaneously, a twenty-three-year-old black man named Philip Kgosana led a silent but defiant march of an estimated 30,000-50,000 men along the 12km route from Langa to Caledon Square police station in Cape Town. They marched in protest of the hated pass laws. From our township street, families watched in fear of what might happen.

I was a year old when the Pass Laws Act of 1952 required Black persons sixteen years and older to carry a domestic passport, commonly called a dompass (a dumb pass) on their person. Each year saw over 250,000 persons arrested for offences related to the dompass. It is telling that the pass law can be traced back to 1760 in the Cape, where the pass was issued to restrict the movement of Black slaves from moving between urban and rural areas. This legislation stopped black South Africans from choosing where they wanted to live. This "restricted living" tied them to the White owner "employers" and formed the bedrock for cheap, exploitative labour.

The Bantustans were part of that legacy that made Black Africans migrants in their own country. Pass law legislation and implementation changed occasionally but remained firmly in place from 1760 until finally repealed in November 1986.

The South African border wars (1966 – 1990)

The South African border wars were in full swing when my two brothers were young. I often heard my father muse angrily, "I'll die before I allow my sons to fight in a war they never started." As wars are, it was an unnecessary conflict, in my father's opinion.

South Africa, during WW1, was part of the British Empire. In 1915, the region known as German Southwest Africa was lost to a defeated Germany. Despite losing its bid to annex the territory, South Africa continued to rule the area from its capital city - Pretoria. Of course, South Africa's Apartheid tsunami prevented black Namibians from having political rights and restricted social and economic freedoms. South Africa's controversial rule over Namibia aimed to exploit its mineral resources[24].

---

24 South African History online
(https://www.sahistory.org.za/article/namibian-struggle-independence-1966-1990-historical-background)

South Africa governed the southwestern region of Southern Africa from 1915 to 1990. South West Africa was like an internal province; the waves of the Apartheid tsunami led to the birth of armed resistance from SWAPO aided by Zambia, Angola and Cuba. This camaraderie is known as the Namibian War of Independence (also known as the Angolan Bush War) and was one of the most significant conflicts on the continent. Why is this relevant, you may ask?

Well, in case you wondered, my dad's father was a second-generation German in Southwest Africa with the surname Smidt. His parents had emigrated from German-Austria. My grandfather settled in Johannesburg after WW1 and, because of political and racial sensitivities at the time, changed his surname to Smith and married a coloured woman, my grandmother, Annie Spilander. They had six children, two daughters and four sons. Two daughters and one brother were fair, while three brothers, including my dad, were shades of "dark". Ah! Sadly, the unity of the indiscriminate, colour-and-ethnic blind world of genetics did not feature in the Apartheid tsunami!

The Apartheid waves – a synoptic scan

South Africa was a safe world for children in those days, and I was nearly five years old when my sister, Carol, arrived. It was also the year that we had to move from Wynberg to Bridgetown on the Cape Flats because of The Group Areas Act.

In a short time, the corrupt system of Apartheid became the tsunami that was to leave a legacy of inhuman abuses legislated by the denizens of political and ethnic power. Ultimately, the racial laws threatened the foundations of South Africa's future.

So, pressurised by circumstances, President FW de Klerk had the intelligence and insight to stem the injustices of his party's Apartheid tsunami. He oversaw the abolishment of legal Apartheid on Friday, 2 February 1990. F. W. de Klerk and Nelson Mandela[25] received the Nobel Prize in 1993 for stopping the historically developed political tsunami. I often wonder if the theologians who justified this corrupt system readily accepted they had manipulated their Bible story. Ah! Human nature.

However, the many years of oppression continued beyond Oslo's acknowledgement that democracy would find root in my motherland. The sad story of the abuse of power continues to make daily news in my corruption-ridden country. The abrogation of discrimination has shown that we, the people of Table Mountain and Kruger National Park fame, still paddle in the mire of the politically engineered framework created by the Apartheid tsunami. Our moral compass has not yet adjusted to embrace respect and equality for all.

My much-loved parents

My story must initially focus on my parents, who loved their children sacrificially and unconditionally. Mom and dad were caring parents who, despite their personal struggles, embedded values that still carry my siblings and me (two boys and four girls) through our own storms. However, to understand my father, we must realise the context of the Apartheid tsunami and its horror.

---

25 Nelson "Madiba" Mandela (1918 – 2013) was a political prison at the Victor Verster Prison, Robben Island and Pollsmoore Prison for a total period of twenty-seven years before his release to become the first democratically elected president of South Africa (1994 – 1999).

Stanley Smith

In 1945, Stanley Smith (my one-of-a-kind dad) returned from WWII with honourable discharge documents in his pocket. In 1948, Stanley, who had patriotically fought for "King and Country", learned that some of his family members were legally reclassified as white. The political waves from the Apartheid tsunami would be an openly divisive force to be reckoned with – within our family.

Dad's siblings called him Buller. He was our Dad. Intelligent, quick and quirky. My first five years of life were filled with wonder and childlike confidence. However, I began to struggle with self-confidence. I was shy and wanted to fade into the colours of the wallpaper when in the company of others. Why was that? There is no doubt that childhood circumstances and Apartheid played a role. As I thought through this, I pictured my dad. His story has its roots in the injustices he, along with countless millions of others, experienced in pre-1994 South Africa.

My father always told us he did not join the army to shoot Germans. He lied about his age, enlisted at seventeen, and was drafted to Egypt. He wanted adventure – to swim in the Mediterranean, climb the pyramids, spend Christmas eve in Cairo, and kiss all the Egyptian girls. He always told us we had stepbrothers and sisters running around in Cairo. That was not a surprise to me. I admired his fascinating wartime pictures and listened to his stories of the pyramids, the Sphinx, and the intrigue of Egypt's magic and mystery. He was a master storyteller to a little girl. I could hear the gruff voice of the evil Captain Hook and see the sun glinting on the curved prosthetic hook while soaring the skies with Peter Pan and Wendy – nightly.

I was fascinated by the tin guitars he made and played. He loved to sing the songs made famous by Vera Lynn and creatively used a glass bottle rolled over the strings to play his version of the Hawaiian guitar. It was beautiful and mournful at the same time.

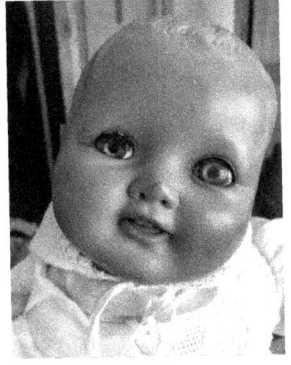

My dad took me to choose my very first doll. My Dulcie was beautiful then and still looks gorgeous seventy years later. However, my girls all think she looks like Chukee with one eye that cannot close anymore. Sadly, they do not want her. However, my youngest granddaughter Halle has promised her a special place in her room and heart.

Stanley and his brothers were known as the Smith brothers. They were a motley bunch who loved to drink and laugh and sometimes fight with each other. In later years, Stanley's drinking sometimes led to alcohol-induced psychosis. We absorbed his mantras into my early nursing career. One day, he knocked a few bricks out of the wall between the main bedroom and our dining room - the influence of one of his regular sundowners! We called it the hole in the wall, and Stanley could watch the newly available TV from his bed.

Life's experiences continued to fuel his cynicism and passive anger. In those days, people of Colour were prohibited from being in "White" areas after working hours. He was going home by bus one night after some drinks with his brothers. He was leaning against a shop window at the bus stop when police approached him. Despite my dad's protestation that he was just waiting for a bus to go home, the young white policemen accused him of "loitering". However, they would let him go if he asked nicely and addressed them as "Baas"[26]. His indignant and steely response to them was, "Baas se moer[27]". He was thrown into the back of the police van and imprisoned. My mother searched hospitals and mortuaries for two weeks. He was in prison but with no right to make a single telephone call.

The wrong platform

I was five years old when I was with my dad on a train to Wittebome, where his sister stayed. I loved those trips to Aunty Sybil because my cousin Iris was my soulmate - two years my senior. Again, my dad defied a white policeman who ordered him to leave the whites-only station platform. Stanley refused to go, and despite my screams, he resisted and fought the disciple of the Apartheid tsunami. I was left alone on the station platform, a terrified and hysterical five-year-old. At the same time, he was thrown into the police van and driven away, and another passenger took me to my aunt's home.

Yes, my dad was a wounded, enraged soul during those years when my siblings were born. He dealt with his mental wounds

---

26 Some racists white males people required non-white people to address them as "baas" – master/boss. The influence of the Dutch invasion of South Africa is noted in the Afrikaans use of "baas", derived from Middle Dutch "baes".
27 An obscene and abusive mode of address, equivalent to 'stuff (you)' of f..k you. Used as an expletive to express rage, disgust, or contradiction.

and rage by drinking and satirical writing. I had many fun-filled learning times in my early years with him – his individualism and unorthodox approach to life captivated my attention. My best times were when he left me sitting in the Railway Café at Cape Town Station, conversing with the staff and regular patrons, while he went to the bar to drink.

The road to independence and other stories

My father taught me to sign my name when I was four. The deal was that he would take me to open my savings account at the post office as soon as I could sign my name. I practised night after night when he came home from work, and when there were no mistakes, he was satisfied.

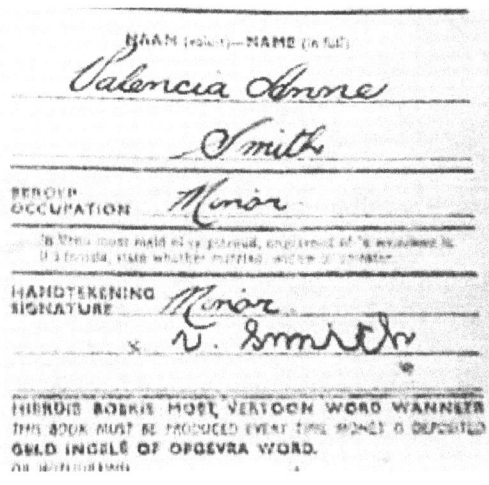

I will never forget the look on the face of the white post office employee, as from the front of the "Non-Whites Only" queue, my dad lifted me and put me on the counter and said to her, "She is here to open a savings account, and will sign her own name." That is still one of the proudest days of my life.

My dad taught me to read and write with chalk on a slate when I was four, long before I started school. He arranged for me to go to school with Rae, our landlord's daughter and a teacher - to sit in the class and learn.

Dad loved photography. Our tiny bathroom, with its bare asbestos ceiling, was turned into a dark room. My dad played around developing his box camera photographs until Kodak hit the market. I would watch him process the small pictures with fascination. He would hand-colour his black and white photos with the gentlest strokes.

The municipality often cut our electricity supply because we could not afford the payments. Cape winters were bad for bricklayers. No work, no pay. However, my resourceful dad would skillfully bypass the security seals in the meter boxes. My mother could cook a meal and boil water when there was no paraffin for the Primus stove. She would cook in the dark so the neighbours would not see the lights burning when they were supposed to be off. Again, it was illegal, but he was living in defiance – and intent on survival - I loved the mesmerising atmosphere of conspiracy.

Stanley was a perfectionist craftsman. Our handmade toys were the envy of other kids. However, while mom had to borrow supper ingredients from neighbours occasionally, our personalized toys were the best – always!

Our scooters had genuine, steel ball-bearing wheels, and we proudly rode the rough streets as the fastest kids on the block.

Our kites were made with precision and pride, with slivers of bamboo adding to his creative touch. Dad could not always afford colour paper, so he used newspapers to launch his creations; our kites flew steadier and higher than any other.

Stanley melted the soles of our plastic school shoes with a candle flame to join the ends when they broke. He taught me how to take off the collar of his shirt when it had frayed, turn it inside out and reattach it - as they did in the army. Consequently, patching a broken garment or a sock with hardly visible crisscross threads became a skill learned from dad's army-taught skills curriculum.

My father had already started to draw plans for a house he envisioned building for my mom and us. I watched in fascination as he sketched his vision, carefully calculated dimensions and the crazy paving pattern for the stoep. I knew every room in that house of paper. However, when the Group Areas Act split families and fragmented communities, he lost interest in making that dream come true. The plans were folded and put away – eventually, nobody knew what had happened to them. However, I learned about reading dimensions, door and window openings and building terms early on. We have some funny stories about me picking up a plan while he and Charles were building and pointing out an error!

My father's creative skills enabled him to build a radio from scratch using old-fashioned valves – another WWII lesson. As a curious preschooler, I had tried to figure out where the person talking was hiding inside those long valves. However, the post-WW II government edited the BBC broadcasts (perceived as biased in favour of the British under Mr and Mrs Windsor). So my dad built his makeshift radio to pick up the BBC! I remember the crackle of the airwaves as he located the right frequency. What he was doing was illegal, and I remember the mystery, the secrecy, and the caution behind it all because of our thin walls. Were any neighbours government-paid informers? Ah, the seeping influence of Jan van Riebeek's 1652 tsunami had begun to morph into divisive nationalism, suspicion, paranoia, resentment and fear of the Afrikaner and other English White conservatives (the powerful in-groups) who controlled and manipulated the Apartheid tsunami to suit their needs and wants.

Change and recognition

Over the years, Dad's binge drinking increased, particularly over weekends. During one of these episodes, while staying with his brother, he fell asleep with a cigarette in his hands. He nearly died that night. I was ten years old when I was taught to change the dressings on the 3rd-degree burns across his back and under his armpits. I would cringe at his pain, but he would urge me to continue. Fortunately, he had an extraordinary nurse in the hospital. She spoke hope into him when he was ready to give up. Her commitment and bedside manner inspired my dream to be a nurse. I was in Standard 2 (Grade 4).

On 31 May 1961, the Union of South Africa became the Republic of South Africa after a Whites-only referendum voted to break away from the United Kingdom. Consequently, during my primary school years, we were required to honour 31 May as

Republic Day. As a ten-year-old learner, I was inducted into the subtle brainwashing all impressionable young people experienced at schools worldwide. The principal held a special assembly for us at our township school. We had no hall, so we stood in the courtyard, freshly scrubbed and excitedly waiting in neat rows with our new gift. The little flag of the Republic of South Africa had replaced the Rooineks'[28] national emblem. I returned home excitedly and told my father about this epic occasion. I thought the flag and ceremony were so cool. However, my dad was not impressed (he was incensed). I fielded his subliminal and verbally blunt messages. After that, I held the new little flag behind my back in school assemblies. With hindsight, I recall the 19th-Century theory of Ivan Pavlov's classical Conditioning Theory that enlightened the forecourts of the social science of politics about the effect of the stimulus and the conditioned reflex - brainwashing.

In 1992, a referendum was held where White South Africans were asked to vote on whether they supported the negotiated reforms announced by President F. W. de Klerk to end legislated apartheid. On 17 March 1992, the results revealed a significant vote for "yes". However, the damage and divisions will still take many decades to heal. Part of that healing is the responsibility of everyone who makes up the church ... this is why Charles and I focus on Christian discipleship.

---

28 The word is taken from Afrikaans to refer to English speaking South Africans – usually of British descent. The word literally means "red-neck" and describes the British Army soldiers whose white pith helmets contrasted with their sunburnt necks. The term was usually used as an insult (https://www.urbandictionary.com/define.php?term=rooinek)

Christ's love controls us (compels us). Since we believe Christ died for all, we also believe that we have all died to our old life[29].

Achievement

Also in 1992, at seventy years of age, dad won a national short story competition and was featured in Tomorrow Magazine. The prize-giving and recognition ceremony venue was an upmarket hotel in Sandton, Johannesburg (some 1,411 km) from Cape Town). So, with the referendum results swirling, my dad and I were flown to Johannesburg for this prestigious event. He looked so dapper that night. My dad was the only brown face amongst other white finalists in the writing category. I used to type his short stories and knew about the rejection and acceptance slips. I was polite and reserved at our table but crumbled emotionally when the Master of Ceremonies announced the writing category winner. Yes, MY dad carried the flag for us "others", and it was such a proud moment for him – and me and our family.

After the eventful night, we were ready for sleep. However, there was a slight complication. Since I was listed as his partner, the room assigned for the night had only one queen-sized bed. I was tired and wanted to get into that beautiful soft bed and sleep. However, my father would not sleep on the same bed as me. I tried every angle of persuasion. He was scared he would roll over and think it was my mom. I countered this and said, "I'll put the pillows between us. How about the suitcase?" Nope. Dad would not budge. I said, "you've had a big night, and we fly back tomorrow. You must sleep." Dad would

---

29 2 Corinthians 5:14.

not comply. "You are one crazy fool, I croaked," and tumbled into the bed. I woke early the following day, and Stanley was sleeping straight up in the desk chair. The empty bottle of complimentary wine, glistening in the morning sunlight, stood on the table next to him.

One of his prizes was a week at a health resort in the beautiful mountains of Mpumalanga, a province 1,700 km from Cape Town. "Well," he said, reading about the prize, "what must I do at that place? Since you do all my typing, I'll ask if I can pass the award on to you and Charles." This was magical. Charles and I could not afford a honeymoon after our marriage. All our other trips away were usually with the children.

Learning about addiction

What a week that was in one of the most beautiful regions of South Africa. Canyons, vistas, waterfalls and rock formations took our breath away. Pilgrim's Rest is a provincial heritage town in the mountains. In 1873 it was the second gold field in the region and attracted a rush of prospectors. It is still a quaint museum town today.

Charles and I arrived at this stunning health farm that provided spas, massages, and guided exercise classes. I could get used to that, I thought. However, I had no idea the food would be rationed to healthy alternatives. No coffee. No cake. No fries. By day three, I started to have caffeine and sugar withdrawal symptoms. Well, at least I learned to empathise with the rabbits – the lettuce and carrots were crunchy.

Nonetheless, Charles is way more disciplined than I am with food choices. When he makes up his mind that he will stop drinking coffee - that is it. He will never touch it again. So, as far as Charles was concerned, we were going to follow the programme to the letter. He had no sympathy for my whining and cravings. So, regressing to being the little child in me, I decided to manipulate Charles. I told him I really wanted to see the sites around Graskop again. He conceded. Yesssss, I thought! Just one pancake from Harry's Pancakes was my destination, and then I could face the rest of the week. As we approached Harry's Pancakes, I said sweetly, "Please let us stop and just taste their pancakes".

No response. Charles kept on driving. "Let us just share one". He kept on going, and I was not a happy companion. In exasperation, Charles agreed to stop at Harry's Pancakes on our way back to the health farm. My sulk and panic subsided, and my mood lifted. On our way back, I grew more excited the closer we got to Harry's Pancakes. Then he did the impossible. He drove right past it. "You just passed it. Did you see the sign?" He ignored me.

Then he said, "We have supper in a short while. We are heading back."

"WHAT? Supper? Leaves and vegetable juices and some fruit and water! I had had it with this detox. My stomach lurched while my mind and body dipped into an emotional quagmire of self-pity.

The tears started in our room, and the flood came – the gushing torrent of tears would have impressed Noah and helped keep the ark afloat! Eventually, Charles said that if I ate my supper, he would slip out clandestinely after the guests had gone to their rooms and go to a local bar at the end of the farm road to get me something sweet to eat. So, come nightfall, he slipped away and took the long walk to find me some contraband chocolate. As I wrote this, I thought of the scripture, "men [and women] love darkness because their deeds are evil![30]" As he selected and received the delectable piece of chocolate cake in a package, a voice behind him said, "That's a long walk you've taken. Tomorrow, we start running at 6 am." The gym instructor from the health farm had caught us out. What a bummer. However, I had never been so happy to share half a chocolate cake with Charles. We both now know something about addiction and devious behaviour. This sugar and chocolate incident was an essential lesson about the importance of empathy. Our future ministry engaged with people needing "fixes" more potent than cocoa beans and sugar cane products. I became acutely aware of the devious methods used to satisfy cravings and could understand their addiction.

When we take visitors on that route, we stop at Harry's Pancakes, and Charles tells our story about the chocolate cake worth eating. I remind him of the "loving darkness" text – a good talking point.

Viva

Dad was seventy-two when I picked him up to cast his vote in the first democratic elections in 1994. He never lost his sharpness of mind and was a brilliant satirist until his death.

On my mother's 60th birthday, Charles, my siblings and I gave our parents a holiday in Canada. They would spend time with a friend from their youth who had emigrated many years before. Mom's cancer had metastasized, but she could still cope with the trip - with stops along the way. A missionary from London

---
30 John 3. 19-21.

City Mission met them in London, checked on her well-being and spent the day taking them around London. In Holland, on the way back, my late sister-in-law Rhoda, studying there, met them and showed them the sites. Rhoda and Stanley got on famously with each other. Stanley found the Red-Light District interesting – he always loved window shopping. They had a wonderful holiday with their friends. My mom would graduate to Heaven five years later.

Dad outlived my mother by ten years. During that time, he finally received the title deed to the house he had rented from the local government for decades. Stanley suffered from mild obstructive airway disease, but his health started to decline when he was diagnosed with leukaemia. It became medically unsafe for him to live alone. He finally agreed to sell up and move in with Charles and me while my brother William built an addition to his home for Dad to spend the remainder of his years.

During the day, he was alone and happy with his books, computer and cigarettes. One day he was surprised by burglars who tied him up, ransacked his room and stole his little cache of cash. They took the only jewellery he had, his wristwatch. However, in true Stanley style, he swiftly but stealthily lifted his watch from the burglar's pocket while they were tying him up. When he demonstrated that for us, we howled with laughter. He spent many days in the hospital during this time. On his 82nd birthday, all his children and grandchildren gathered at William and Bevvy's home, and we partied as only the Smith clan know.

With his last hospital admission after his 82nd birthday, Charles and I had the privilege of placing his hand in Jesus' hand. At the same time, he lay in the hospital bed. He always said that Jesus and he had a special relationship because he was a bricklayer and Jesus was a carpenter. I am sure they did have a special relationship, and I thanked him for being our father.

Stanley was loved. "You've done a good job with us," I told him. "We're going to be OK." He was discharged from the hospital and died a few weeks later while sleeping in his bed and room. We held the funeral service at William's home – not in a church building. Stanley had left us. With his children and grandchildren gathered around, we celebrated and shared memories from pictures. Just like he would have wanted it. No fuss and pomp!

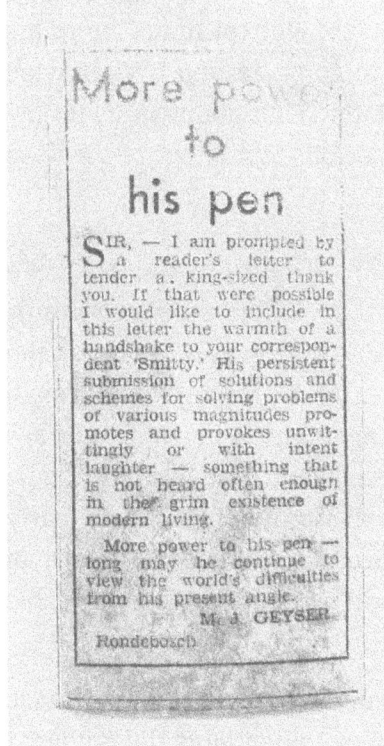

Dad was quiet when he was sober, always a thinker, but garrulous when he was drunk. He was intelligent, creative, witty, and loved writing short stories. He was a master satirist and would take stabs at the Apartheid regime by writing letters to the editor of the Cape Argus. They called him the man with the golden pen. I still have some of his stories and letters. This publication is part of my commitment to sharing these precious memories. My sisters and I will share dad's writings with our children and grandchildren. I still love the rustle, smell, and contents of the faded yellow papers and his letters.

How many generations will lose the joy of rummaging and retrieving history from family archives?

Emails will never replace what I still experience when handling those fragile bits of paper. My sister Vivie and I found one letter he wrote home from Egypt. We cautiously laid open the flimsy writing paper and read about the Egyptian girl who told dad (the young soldier), "You don't have to die to go to heaven." We howled with laughter so many decades later. That about sums up my awesome dad - the unique and precious Stanley.

Thelma Engelbrecht

My mother, Thelma, is the story of a different soul. She was everything that my father was not. Her calm character and genteel ways remain fixed in my mind. Orphaned at the age of two, she was raised by an aunt who became the grandmother of my early years. Grandma's house in suburban Newlands tickled the base of Table Mountain.

I would travel unaccompanied from Bridgetown to her house with "E4 to Kirstenbosch" written on paper. Mom did not want me to board the wrong bus; the world was a relatively safer place for kids then.

Ma Lenie's house and apron carried the tempting aroma of freshly baked bread and delicious tapioca pudding. Ma Lenie seemed so old to a little girl like me. I was never close to her aloof husband. After he died, I continued to visit and spend weekends and holidays at the foot of the impressive Table Mountain. I would lie down to sleep next to her in her big, high old bed with the unique aroma of home cooking reminding me of everything tasty. I would watch her chest rise and fall until I, too, fell asleep. She seemed so old that I thought she would die in her sleep. Was this custom preparing me for future losses when my God and the Apartheid tsunami would disturb my rest?

Paradise lost

My childhood friend Geoffrey lived a few houses down from Ma Lenie. I learned to ride a bicycle in his yard. I picked up many scars and scrapes on my legs, knees and elbows while perfecting a turn! Aunty Henna lived next door to Geoffrey's house. I had access to extra delicious and fresh baked bread and tasty homemade jam from the fruit trees in the garden. Little did I know that the turbulent waves of the Apartheid tsunami would soon disrupt this community. Families would be uprooted and scattered to the outer perimeters of this idyllic setting nestling at the foot of one of the world's most fantastic tourist attractions.

Heritage and Thelma

My mother did not have an easy life, but she never lost her

grace and fortitude. Mom was always the lady - old-fashioned[31] in her views about children and elders (kids may be seen but not heard[32]). Mom was more of the disciplinarian in my early years. She hated backchat. I had a dinner plate cracked over my head once for being cheeky. After that, I always stood far enough away whenever I tried to make my case during future altercations. Mom was fastidious about respect and table etiquette, and her unique English mannerisms reflected the English influence of the 1820 Settlers in her life. Her Thelmarisms (as we sisters called it) dictated how we should hold a teacup, when milk must be added to tea and how warm it should be. Of course, the position of a knife and fork on a plate was a sign of socially approved etiquette a-la-Britannia. In contrast, my down-to-earth father could not care less about that pomp.

Trips to the seaside

Thelma packed our beach gear when dad took us to Kalk Bay. Stanley resented the Apartheid law limiting him to only Kalk Bay. However, that was the only section of beach that coloured families could go to in those years. We travelled by bus and train. Dad and mom had countless pictures of

---

31 Generally referring to English customs – etiquette.
32 Now judged as "unacceptable" by 21st-Century standards of childcare.

themselves on other beaches before they were declared only for whites. The concept of loss was to become a pattern during my adult life.

I loved looking at those youthful pictures of my parents – they were a happy couple. Of course, dad always took his wine with him during visits to Kalk Bay. Alcohol enabled him to manage the justified resentments he carried.

Mom seldom accompanied us on our Kalk Bay beach outings – maybe she needed time to recharge her emotional batteries. However, just as the high tides would change the contours of the beach, Apartheid's tsunami was soon to impose more changes on South Africa. My God would disturb me, and the spectrum of loss would become a force that would cause me to seek refuge in the Rock of Ages.

Decades later, we siblings took our children to Kalk Bay on a train. We wanted them to know that part of our story. They enjoyed the train ride but did not think much of Kalk Bay as a beach. After all, they had their pick of the best beaches the Cape offers by this time. Happily, the "Whites only" signs and "No Non-whites and dogs" signs no longer stopped anyone (or animal) from enjoying swimming, frolicking in the water and building sandcastles.

The Big C

My mother was diagnosed with breast cancer when I started nursing. Her faith battle and fighting spirit, as she lived with cancer for the next twenty-five years, inspired my hope when I was diagnosed with breast cancer many decades later. My youngest sibling was so little then. I remember bargaining with God for my mother's life … "Please God, just until Vivie…" and

He kept giving her extensions! Little did I know, He would continue to disturb me as I grew older – the waves from the Apartheid tsunami were on their way – to barrel into me and impact those I loved.

Table Mountain

However, it was under Table Mountain's canopy that the threads of my story began to weave into the events that would influence my life in another direction – very soon. Chapter 2 will focus on the footprints of a unique and humble Christ follower – a foreigner from the United Kingdom. His focus contrasted with the preying commercialism of the Dutch East India Company and the arrival of strangers who tramped across the white, sandy beaches. Sadly, this otherwise idyllic setting beneath the magnificent tablecloth that often drapes our globally-known mountain belies the injustices and horror that ignored the First People. The Apartheid tsunami would callously romp unchecked across South Africa. However, a thread of hope would soon weave a pattern of hope at the hands of one man – a gentleman and Christian from the United Kingdom.

Chapter Two

Frederick George Lowe, Portuguese Footprints, Jan van Riebeek and Colonial Chicanery

My story has a strange twist, and I must begin to unravel the threads that led to my career. After introducing Frederick George Lowe, the founder of the City Slum Mission[33], I must set the sociopolitical and economic stage.

F. G. Lowe – he went about doing good

My faith, career and ministry have much to do with this saintly man. He was one of the many who followed in the wake of the 1820 Settlers that Britain sent to Cape Town. Mr Lowe (aware of the work of the renowned London City Mission) pioneered the City Slum Mission. Its Gospel outreach began at the base of Table Mountain.

---

33 Later to be known as the Cape Town City Mission.

So, when I reluctantly and with trepidation took over the leadership of the Cape Town City Mission in 2008, I desperately needed to know about the original founding philosophy of its founder, Frederick George Lowe, born in 1852. I began researching his life in archived material in state libraries and newspapers. His ethical values, love for the poor and outcast of the city, commitment to doing good, and refusal to take any credit for what he did set him apart from the fame seekers and egoists with clay feet. Brother Lowe used to sit with the needy and, while sharing the Gospel, would serve them wherever he found them. He lived the discipling legacy of Jesus Christ, and the pioneering work he began 120 years ago introduced many people to the message of salvation. This message eventually reached me.

While the restored grave lies in a forgotten part of a Cape Town cemetery, the Gospel message he proclaimed and his blameless life impacted people. Just as the trees at the foot of Table Mountain provided their fruit for that tasty fruit jam of my childhood, the threads from Lowe's faith and works continue to meet the needs of people in Cape Town today. Sadly, no monuments are named after him; the name on his new gravestone says nothing of his greatness, grace and stature. The epitaph, written by his sisters who stayed in Nottingham (UK), simply reads, "He went about doing good".

F. G. Lowe lived the concept of servant leadership. I have often wondered about the story of the Nottingham resident, Robin Hood, who, according to legend, robbed the rich to serve the poor. Were there leaves and twigs from Sherwood Forest in the life and witness of Frederick George Lowe?

Portuguese footprints (15th – 17th Centuries)

The Portuguese were the first Europeans to enter Africa when Henry the Navigator and Bartolomeu Dias left their footprints on the continent. Pêro de Alenquer rounded the southern tip, naming it the Cape of Storms. He ironically renamed it the Cape of Good Hope on his return trip. The Portuguese used South Africa as a junction to engage in the local slave trade and outflank Islam, which was also involved in slavery and was a competitor for the minds and souls of people. They left stone crosses and Roman Catholic missionaries behind them to convert the inhabitants to Christianity – while simultaneously selling people at the market. Their missionary endeavours remain dotted across the country. The southern tip of Africa was a halfway stop for their trade links with India.

However, the trade-hungry entrepreneurs of the Netherlands also used the Cape of Good Hope as a strategic place from which they could control European trade with China. They would benefit from the lucrative African slave trade and wrest control from the Portuguese, who had a powerful influence over the Indian Ocean. The vehicle they used was the Dutch East India Company, and Jan van Riebeek was its first emissary to Cape Town.

Jan van Riebeek and Table Mountain

Now we will turn to the substance of the political tsunami that Jan van Riebeek initiated in 1652. He orchestrated the welcome for the arrival of Dutch Settlers who, with their unique socio-cultural and political legacy, would begin to settle under the shadow of Table Mountain. The influx of foreign influence would be compounded when the 1820 Settlers arrived from England with their different perceptions of "how things must be done".

The Great Trek – a synopsis

The Dutch settlers decided to move north – the Great Trek began between 1835 and 1840s. Some 12,000 - 14,000 Boers[34] migrated northwards to escape from British rule. They defeated the Xhosa peoples, reached Natal and the Highveld, and established white settlements north of the Limpopo River. Afrikaners[35] regard The Great Trek as the core event of their 19th-century history and the origin of their nationhood. This sociopolitical earthquake caused the turbulence that gave birth to the Apartheid tsunami that flooded South Africa in 1948. The land-grabbing from the First Peoples by the Dutch, British and Voortrekkers was to reap bitter fruit.

Colonial chicanery

The rolling political-cultural tsunami of colonialism introduced by the British reinforced the concept of European social

---

34 Afrikaners (Boers) - the descendants of European (Dutch, German, and French) colonists, indigenous Khoisan peoples, and African and Asian slaves in the Dutch colony at the Cape of Good Hope. They spoke the West Germanic language of South Africa. (https://www.britannica.com/topic/Afrikaans-language).
35 Descendants of the Dutch settlers.

structuring[36] under successive governments and the eventual birth of the United Party[37] in South Africa. The United Party ruled between 1934 and 1948 when the rival (Whites-only National Party) brandished its political tsunami's crest, and "Rule Britannia" was no longer welcome at the table. The hold on power by the minority Whites-only cabal remained entrenched in an already culturally divided country. The First People and others who were not classified as "White" remained the underdogs. The Apartheid tsunami was beginning its destructive surge across southern Africa.

With the gift of hindsight, I now understand how, following the 1652 toe-in-the-water arrival of the colonial administrator of the Dutch East India Company[38], Jan van Riebeek, also heralded the future British colonisation of South Africa. British imperialism and the systematic blanking of indigenous cultures became the norm.

The flagrant disregard for the First People had begun at the southern tip of Africa at the foot of the magnificent Table Mountain – the epicentre of the Apartheid tsunami. So it was that my dad, with other First Nation and some Settler people, became unwilling vassals of a Biblical ideology according to the National Party's theologians. So, the warped religious mindset

---

36 Probably emanating from the feudal system that took root in England when William of Normandy conquered King Harold in 1066, flourished in Medieval Europe from the 9th to the 15th centuries and accentuated during the Victorian Era (1837-1901) when the British Empire was at its colonising peak and the sun never set on its Empire.
37 Formed by a merger of most of Prime Minister Barry Hertzog's National Party with the rival South African Party of Jan Smuts, plus the remnants of the Unionist Party.
38 With the start of the western colonization in the 15th century South Africa was initially colonised by the Netherlands and then Great Britain. The Dutch East India Company actively facilitated the colonial ambitions of Britain. Britain experienced a serious unemployment problem after the Napoleonic Wars and in 1820 sent the first group of settlers to the Cape Colony and some then went to what is now known as Port Elizabeth. The waves from the political tsunami began to spread.

that sullied the social, cultural, political network and educational content of South Africa was personified in the actions of the denizens of inhumane apartheid ideology. Similarly, Hitler's Mein Kampf marketed his manifesto for the Nazi Party. This evil dogma led to his virulent antisemitic views, his classification of the "Untermenschen", and the Holocaust.

As a child, I had not understood the full implications of Apartheid. Still, naiveté was to give way to harsh realities and cognitive appraisal – voila, critical thinking.

Whereas Frederick George Lowe came to share the message of the Christian Gospel and integrated with the poor and needy, other strangers from across the sea, from culturally different backgrounds, had another agenda. In pursuit of their self-centred goals, they ignored the culture and rights of the First People of South Africa. Colonising greed and thirst for absolute power paved the way for van Riebeek's[39] political-economic enterprise to grow into the Apartheid tsunami. Paradoxically, the hallowed precincts of Table Mountain became the epicentre from which the evils of Apartheid began to spread.

The ideological and commercialised ravaging of the rights of the First People by foreigners will feature briefly in the following chapter. Readers will get a glimpse of the spawning of the hideous Apartheid tsunami that was to leave scars on the citizens of the changing face of South Africa. This narrative will show how an endemic of misplaced self-serving nationalism, financial greed and the ever-present power dynamic buried the right to the franchise of most people in the country.

---

39 Acting under the Dutch East India Company.

Chapter Three

The rise of settler-originated nationalism and the Apartheid tsunami

In 1948 Daniel Francois Malan[40] became Prime Minister of South Africa. The electorate voted out the United Party and welcomed the National Party, which comprised the offspring of those descendants that had formed part of van Riebeek's commercial visit to Cape Town.

The Apartheid tsunami

The National Party swept into office, winning eighty seats (predominantly from Afrikaner voters) compared to the United Party's sixty-four seats[41].

Their forced legalised "Whites Only" policy infiltrated and impaired South Africa's diverse social, cultural and economic bastions. So, legally disenfranchised the majority of South Africans (who were not "white"). The cold-hearted Apartheid ideology had edited the country's collage of socio-political,

---

40 Malan completed his Doctor of Divinity at the University of Utrecht in 1905 and was ordained as a minister of the Dutch Reformed Church. His strong Afrikaner nationalism led him into the arena of politics.
41 Black History: https://www.blackpast.org/global-african-history/apartheid-1948-1994/ [Accessed 5 October 2022].

cultural and economic fibres. White nationalists undemocratically dominated and divided South Africa to suit their needs and wants. Subsequently, from 1948 to 1994, the contentiously polluted waves from the Apartheid tsunami continued to erode justice, evade accountability, stymie social development and inhibit economic growth for most people of South Africa[42]. Apartheid poisoned education and truncated employment and career opportunities for those legislated as "other than white". Its laws uprooted and divided families, interfering with the personal and social lives of people who loved each other.

While Hitler and his thugs had created ghettos for "others" – the so-designated "Untermenschen[43]" - the Nationalist Regime had created Group Areas and separate but equal opportunities (sic) for others. The destructive Apartheid tsunami swept South Africa's cultural, social, economic and political landscape. The human cost is evidenced in the psychological, mental and physical scars that remain – and lie within graves. Many families do not know where the bodies of their loved ones have been buried.

Resistance – a synoptic glimpse

In 1948 in Johannesburg, the Transvaal Indian Congress (TIC) instituted their "Decade of Defiance" and anti-pass laws[44] demonstrations that saw the burning of passes in Port

---

[42] Whites, who comprised 20% of the nation's population, would continue to dominate the country (Ibid Black History).

[43] Hitler's theory of unternmenschen (sub-humans) was the regime's philosophy that the Germans and people of Germanic descent were superior to all other races on earth.

[44] People classified as "black" had to carry a document – the Pass. Failing to present this document led to a fine. My thoughts to the Jews during Hitler's rampage across Germany – they had to wear the Star of David whenever they left their house.

Elizabeth. The Nationalist regime responded harshly, and legally protected reprisals followed.

In March 1950, the African National Congress proclaimed 1 May as Freedom Day. All organisations were called to participate in widespread demonstrations and the call for full franchise rights for all. In 1951, Nelson Mandela was elected president of the African National Congress Youth League (ANCYL). The anti-Apartheid tsunami movement earned popular support amongst the disenfranchised, and many White comrades enlisted. Opposition to the looming Group Areas Act led to the call for a general strike. Police opened fire in Alexandra Township and other surrounding areas killing eighteen people and wounding thirty more. Brutality, counterattacks, and oppression featured throughout the struggle for democracy - mirroring the actions taken by the Nazis during their rise to and hold on power.

Separation and violence

On 12 May 1950, The Immorality Amendment Act No 21 1950[45] ruptured my dad's family, splitting the family unit. On 7 July 1950, The Group Areas Act, Act No 41 of 1950[46], was passed. This heinous legislation, enacted a year before my birth, would eventually play a divisive role in my life and destiny. Ultimately, the politically encultured violence of the Apartheid tsunami would become a conscious reality.

Yes, the Dutch East India Company had changed the lives of The First People and others in South Africa. Yes, their

---

[45] The Act was to amend the Immorality Act, 1927, "so as to prohibit illicit carnal intercourse between Europeans and non-Europeans, and to provide for matters incidental thereto."
[46] The Group Areas Act No 41 forced physical separation and segregation between races by creating different residential areas for each designated race.

colonising influence would spawn violence. Paradoxically, my life would be changed for the better by a 2000-year-old act of violence. A Roman executioner had mercilessly hammered nails into the wrists and feet of Jesus Christ. Consequently, I found a relationship of trust in my God of grace, who protected and guided me to fulfil the plan He had prepared before the foundation of the world (c.f. Chapter 4).

The following chapter will focus on my reality of the rise of the Apartheid tsunami in the 1950s and the 1966 events, which in one sense, foreshadowed the ultimate cycle of endemic political brutality. The legal framework for Apartheid came from the minds of individuals whose blinkered vision rested between a ridiculous theological belief and an exclusive "Whites Only" nationalistic goal.

Apartheid was, in one sense, the archetype of the historical laager. The Boer wagons had formed a protective circle around the foreign settlers who forcibly displaced those with the right to their land. Brief pen pictures of these individuals feature in the following chapter.

Chapter Four

The active planners of the Apartheid tsunami and the plan of the Cross

Dr H. F. Verwoerd (a Dutch descendant) was the Prime Minister of South Africa from 1958-1966 and was initially the chief editor of Die Transvaler Newspaper[47]. He was a scholar of applied psychology and sociology and is commonly regarded by some as the architect who refined and socially constructed the Apartheid[48] tsunami.

On 6 September 1966, at around 13:00, I arrived home from school, and my mother was glued to the radio. Dr Verwoerd was dead - assassinated in the House of Parliament[49]. My mother, this graceful, reserved woman, shrieked with delight. I shook my head in disbelief at her reaction to this news. It

---

47 The first attempt to assassinate Dr Verwoerd by David Pratt (by shooting in 1960) was unsuccessful. The second attempt, by Dimitri Tsafendas (by stabbing in 1966) was successful.
48 Arguably, Verwoerd, of Dutch descent gave impetus and structure to the official policy of successive Dutch and British colonial administrations (as noted earlier in this book). Malan, Strijdom and other white nationalists had tinkered around the edges until brutally enforced by Verwoerd.
49 The first assassination attempt was made on the life of Prime Minister H.F. Verwoerd at the Rand Easter Show in Johannesburg. His assailant was a disgruntled White farmer, David Pratt, who fired two shots at the Minister at close range. Despite two bullets in his head, he miraculously escaped death (https://www.sahistory.org.za/dated-event/there-assassination-attempt-verwoerd-rand-easter-show-johannesburg).

seemed so incongruous, and I was embarrassed that I had heard and seen her response to this news. She tried to explain that the engineer of the hideous Apartheid tsunami had been murdered. She kept telling me that he was a bad man. Years later, I understood how deep my parent's pain had been during those wicked times.

My God's plan

Two months later, I was a fifteen-year-old teenager. I attended a church service on that memorable Wednesday night (23 November 1966). The event of that night changed the course and direction of my life. For the first time, I understood the message of the Cross when a man I regard as my spiritual father, Bruce Duncan, revealed God's heart to me. I began to discover my God and how He would always be at my back and remain my shepherd. Bruce Duncan would continue to teach me about faith in a miracle-working God and love for the poor and outcast. That night my life changed, and my heart exploded because of the finished work of Christ on the Cross. For me!

Fifty-six years later, I can still see and feel every detail of that faith encounter where, as a 15-year-old girl, I was sobbing my way into a new life in Christ. I had no idea of the faith adventures that lay ahead. I had no idea that the young lad, Charles Kadalie, playing the guitar in the Kadalie Boys' band, would become my husband. I had no idea of my God's incredible people who would serve as spiritual mentors and role models in the coming decades.

My spiritual awakening upset my mother. I could not understand her tears and displeasure. However, she had mistakenly thought I was telling her that her religious denomination was not good enough and soon came to faith in Christ. On the other hand, my father was not a formal religious acolyte. He loved spirituality and the concept of a Creator God but did not love the organisation called "the church". He loved the cosmos, stars and telescopes, which triggered his endearment with science fiction. With his entrenched cynicism, Stanley gave me three months before I would throw off "this religious garbage". Then he gave me until I was sixteen, then eighteen, and then twenty-one. He finally accepted that his God of all creation was also part of my life!

Everything began to take on a new perspective. Three years later, when I was eighteen and six months into my nursing studies, I met Charles at my friend's birthday party. Little did I know that my God would assign Charles as my life partner. We would become parents of two precious daughters, a son by adoption, five grandchildren and many spiritual children – and wonderful special friends.

Charles Kadalie

I was my quiet eighteen-year-old self when Charles walked into my friend's home. The room was happily pulsating with birthday noise, and he just took over. The church football players were all there, and I was the club secretary. Charles, an extrovert, was boisterous, noisy and funny. He got my attention just because it was hard not to notice him. His quick and witty retorts made me smile. He still describes exactly what I wore that night. I, the introvert, shrank into the wall - we met again five weeks later at my home on my nineteenth birthday. The introvert soon began to reach out and scrape herself from the wall!

My mother, ever the lady, offered Charles and the other boys tea. Charles took over the room again and began to charm his way into my mother's heart. Maybe my mom loved him before I knew I did.

Twenty years later, my mother wanted me to get Charles some tea while she lay dying in a hospital bed. Charles promised her he would go and buy some tea when his workday ended. I let my siblings and my father know how terminal my mom was. Charles, my siblings and I sat around her deathbed with my father - sipping the tea Charles had bought. I am sure she knew that and was happy. You never left Thelma's home without tea. So, we all had our "cuppa" before she left her sick bed and us to enter her new, Apartheid-free home on Valentine's Day 1990.

Soon after my 19th birthday, Charles and I started seeing each other whenever possible. However, his parents were much stricter than mine – extremely authoritarian and religious. I was not used to that. In our home, there was alcohol around most weekends, and my father had very different religious views. He and his two younger brothers gave us glimpses of a colourful life when they had drinks together. Consequently, Charles and I went to many soccer matches to meet in the stands and enjoy being together and away from stern "dating warnings" at his home.

A cold night – and consequences

Our youth group often climbed Table Mountain, and I was studying Psychiatric nursing. I decided on a break to join our student group, which went climbing with Charles (of course!). The meandering paths and solitude allowed time for bonding and refuge away from the hassles of everyday life – and the prying eyes of parents. However, we got caught in a sudden weather change on the way down the mountain. None of us had prepared for this freak change of weather. We had no warm clothing. We were suddenly trapped in a podgy grey blanket of mist, and the cheerful sun had beat a hasty retreat – we were trapped in a gloomy, icy cocoon. There were no mobile phones. Charles and I took charge.

I remembered that my father loved the majestic Table Mountain - his sanctuary from the gnawing irritants that plagued him. He had always told us that if the weather suddenly changed while on the mountain, we must stay put and not move. Respect the mountain, he drummed into me. We did just that. Yes, that early ability to trust is still my way of thinking, and I have discovered that my trust in my Lord and Saviour keeps me secure.

The group had been split in two at different sections of the path. "Stay put and huddle up to the person in front and behind you. It will be freezing, but we'll have to sit this out. Keep talking and singing," Charles shouted through the damp enveloping mist. Charles and I spent the night on the mountain, and the Welsh Choir could not hold a candle to our choral recitals! Regardless of our singing abilities, Charles and I were not married. We were spending the night on the mountain – for some, this was food for juicy gossip!

However, we returned safely in all our innocence to the base of tourism's icon the following day, and Charles took me home. My parents were so relieved, and my dad was delighted we had followed his advice. However, Charles' father visited my home that morning and was NOT happy! He gave my dad a mouthful because I had dared to spend the night out with his son.

"Fenner, don't be a damned fool," my father said, dismissing the conversation.

From one group to another – the Cape Town City Mission

As a group of young people who loved music, football, and youth work, we often met at the Kadalie home where Charles, his brothers and one sister lived. I would be reminded of my God's pre-vision four decades later when I needed help for Lisa. I started going with them to the Cape Town City Mission in Smart Street, District 6. By now, I had left the Christian denomination of my youth because I had been baptised as a believer in water - the elders consequently expelled me. I suppose I could call it constructive dismissal! Fortuitously, the Cape Town City Mission did not have a problem with this step of obedience. So it was that the developing outcomes of the founding work of Frederick George Lowe became my spiritual home. Many subsequently contributed to its ministry of "faith and works". They unknowingly shaped and moulded me to fit into my ministry with Charles. I got to know and love District 6, and, above all, Charles was born there, and that is where I studied midwifery.

I celebrated my twentieth birthday during the rough times when the Apartheid bulldozers rolled across District 6. With an indiscriminate focus, the giant juggernauts of destruction flattened homes, churches, and, of course, my beloved Cape Town City Mission meeting halls. Families were subsequently scattered across the sandy wastes of the Western Cape and were shoehorned into brick-and-mortar "houses". The loss and bereavement experienced by individuals uprooted from their homes and society and their unbelievable emotional pain added to their confusion, fear, family instability and social problems. This violent uprooting will take generations to heal. Just as the victims of the Nazi Holocaust, the victims of the Apartheid-driven tsunami still carry the scars of this racist edict. Hopefully, learned academics bent on adding a doctorate to their CV might yet research and publish the socioeconomic and psychological aftermath that dogged the steps of the "resettled".

Nonetheless, the Cape Town City Mission leaders followed the displaced families into the various parts of the Cape Flats to set up church communities in people's homes. This practice was akin to how the early church began[50]. Undoubtedly, the relevance of the 21st-century witness of the Cape Town City Mission remains the responsibility of its 21st-century leaders.

Ministry and the church

I recall Aunty Bella and Uncle Johnny Lightburn, who, during my psychiatric nursing stint, had offered their tiny one-roomed flat as our base. Unexpectedly, before their turn came to give way to the bulldozers, Charles and I helped my father-in-law with their funeral. They were spared the trauma of Apartheid's tsunami-enforced relocation.

We knew so little, but we learned so much. We had no formal theological training, but we had incredible Christian mentors in leaders like Bruce Duncan, Pat Kelly, Fenner Kadalie and Alec Kadalie. Consequently, like those who came to take over our land in 1652 and 1820, we too pioneered our new roads through the wastelands – while facing the waves of the

---

50 Acts 2.46.

inescapable Apartheid tsunami engineered by Dominee[51] D. F. Malan.

We followed the last of the District 6 families to Hanover Park. Ma Wassung and her family had moved to Hanover Park during these awful years. We started working from her tiny council house. The church[52] grew, and our learning continued. We learned from our people's resilience, tenacity, and unique humour. They battled to carve a new life for their families amid a strange, sandy environment that contrasted with the paved roads and pavements of Whites Only infrastructure.

Charles and I still engage with the fourth generation of these pioneers who were forced to live in areas where sand, concreted roads and boxed houses looked across to Table Mountain. We are well out of sight and mind to those who gawk at the Malay Quarter and its quaint, brightly coloured houses and cobbled streets. Did those travelling in the Table Mountain cable car comprehend the parody of discriminatory contradictions beneath their feet?

Chapter 5 focuses on how Charles and I took voluntary day admission to a hospital for the mentally ill. I faced the lapping waves of the Apartheid tsunami that impacted patients undergoing electroconvulsive therapy (ECT). Of course, external forces challenged Charles and me. I will share how my God helped us walk through the deluge of ill health. We will resurrect the protectionist defences in the municipality and how we took the initiative to successfully challenge the old boy

---

51 The Dutch title Dominee is the equivalent title of "Reverend", "Father", "Priest".
52 The word "church" derives from the Greek – εκκλησία. Church, originally meant an assembly called out by the magistrate, or by legitimate authority. It was in this last sense that the word was adapted and applied by the writers of the New Testament to the Christian congregation. So, the church now meets in buildings. The believers of those called out by God.

networks. The chapter ends with the powerful words of Sir Harold "Supermac" MacMillan, the pragmatic and insightful British Prime Minister who upset the South African government.

Chapter Five

Crossing the Rubicon – reality and empathy

While working as a qualified psychiatric nurse during the early days of our life together (not on Table Mountain!), I took off my profession's epaulettes. On my special request, I obtained permission to be a voluntary patient in a psychiatric unit for six weeks from 0600 to 2200 daily. I wanted to understand what it felt like to be a patient in a psychiatric ward. That experience changed my life and my perspectives on roles, titles, power and position. I learned about compassion – empathy. The impact of the Apartheid tsunami swirled in those alien surroundings where I could not spend the nights because of Apartheid laws. I was legally classified as Coloured, while the other patients were White.

Charles would fetch me every night to take me home. I do not remember a night that I did not just flood the car and his shoulders with my tears. We had to get married in a few weeks, and he thought I was falling apart! He was furious and insisted that I give up and stop the experiment. I would weep and scream, "NO! I must see it through. I am learning so much. I can't stop now!" Eventually, one night I said to him, "You won't understand unless you do it yourself." To my amazement, he took me seriously and said, "Well then, you see that you organise the placement. I am going to be a patient too". I had two weeks left, and thanks to a progressive and amazing psychiatric team, Charles spent those two weeks as a patient with me – he, too, understood. Oh my, we had no idea what our God had up his sleeve for us.

Charles and I learned about empathy. We have drawn on that store of compassion in our lives and ministry. Other lessons have strengthened us. We learned about pride and vulnerability and understood the barriers we set to protect ourselves in relationships with others. We recognised the healthy and unhealthy ways of responding to life's challenges and the healing power of expressing anger and not suppressing it. We discovered the road to responsible concern and the power of forgiving yourself and others – yes, our Lord was indeed preparing us. We saw the value of making friends with the past and recognised the magic of humour and laughter and learning to laugh at oneself.

A thread from a different source

As an aside, while drafting this story, one person mentioned in this narrative told me that part of his psychology module at the University of South Africa[53] entailed observation visits to a mental hospital. Under the guidance of a psychiatrist, he had witnessed electroconvulsive therapy in the Apartheid-divided Coloured and White sections of the hospital. The White patients received an anaesthetic before the ECT took place. On the non-white side, patients waiting for their ECT had to lie on beds in a huge ward. One-by-one, the trolley with the apparatus

---

53 Today UNISA communicates online and not solely by pigeon post.

passed down the row of beds. Each patient received a jolt of electricity (without a sedative). Those who waited their turn watched their fellow patients convulsing as the current jolted through them. Of course, they had a gag to bite on so they would not bite their tongue. He was told by the psychiatrist that the sedative was too expensive for "these people."

I witnessed and assisted at many ECT sessions during my training. The use of anaesthetics and muscle relaxants was widespread by the late 1950s. Regardless, this unmodified ECT was still used during my training in the 1970s. At least four of us had to hold all the long bones of our patients to prevent fractures and injury during treatment! I was so scared when Lisa had to have ECT forty-eight years later.

The waves from a discriminatory, inhumane Apartheid tsunami lapped the floorboards of a hospital caring for the mentally ill – and irony upon ironies, my God, was going to remind me of this specific issue.

Tying the knot

Charles and I married in March of 1976 when I turned twenty-five. I would have loved to marry at twenty-one but feared my future in-laws, and we were both studying.

Our fellow patients were guests at our wedding. How special that was!

Charles always says it took four ministers to tie the knot. Bruce Duncan, Fenner Kadalie (my father-in-law), Pat Kelly and Uncle Alec!

However, I was late for my wedding because my father was tipsy and refused to put on his shoes. He said Charles could wait until he wanted to walk me down the aisle! He needed another drink first. After all, he was about to suffer another significant loss – his eldest daughter.

We tied a tight knot

Alarmingly, Charles got quite ill just a few months before our wedding. He developed Tuberculosis of the spine that was not detected immediately until they decided to drain a psoas abscess in his groin. For the first few months leading into our marriage, I had to ensure he took his daily medication and administered daily injections. So we had an out-of-the-ordinary start to our marriage – but this was another thread that would link me to ...

Charles had lost a lot of weight by the time he had donned his wedding suit! Miraculously, he had no spinal damage and recovered fully - until his brush with asbestos twenty-one years later. What a campaign that turned out to be!

Testing the knot and learning

We had moved house the year before when, in 1997, Charles developed a distressing cough that would not clear. In fact, he felt so sick that we decided not to go to our family GP but to find a doctor in our new neighbourhood. The new doctor took a comprehensive medical history from Charles. When this "in touch" doctor heard about Charles' years of power station work, he ordered immediate X-Rays.

Charles had been in the electrical field in power stations for most of his professional career. The hazards of asbestos were officially known in these circles of power. Perhaps, it was expedient for the powers sitting behind desks on carpeted floors not to disclose this hazard. Maybe health and safety laws were not as advanced as they are today. Maybe, it was best not to rock the boat. However, our God orchestrated things for us, including our timeous introduction to Neolife nutrition. Charles is alive today as one of the longest-surviving victims of asbestosis.

Asbestosis has a very long latency period in the lungs. The first symptoms typically appear ten to twenty years after the initial exposure. What would have made that doctor immediately consider an occupational disease like asbestosis?! We believe it was our God. The x-rays gave us cause for alarm, and Charles was referred to a thoracic surgeon. A thoracotomy was scheduled. The doctors thought he had mesothelioma – an aggressive lung cancer caused by asbestos. We prepared ourselves for the bad news that part of his affected lung may have to be removed to save his life. I knew he was in serious trouble. My God was the only one I felt safe turning to. He heard my cry. Yes, the lung lining was severely scarred and would never heal, but it had not progressed to mesothelioma.

Charles-a-la-Tutankhamun

Charles was discharged, and two weeks into recovery at home, he was in bed when I left for work. It was on a rainy winter's morning on the national road leading into Cape Town. The traffic had come to a standstill, so I was stationary. I saw headlights fast approaching in my rear-view mirror and realised that this driver would be unable to stop in time. I could not take any evasive action. Then everything happened in slow motion, yet at breakneck speed. The approaching car swerved, and I saw it flash past my window. At the same instant, the car behind him smashed right into the back of my car. My vehicle crashed into the back of a stationary police van in front of me. My car was a write-off, and I was dazed but unscathed. I had no option but to call Charles on his recovery bed. I needed to know what to do. I could not think straight. He told me to stay put and came to my rescue with his bandaged chest, giving a glimpse into what Tutankhamun might have looked like without the ornate headdress.

When he was ready to return to work, the thoracic surgeon had warned Charles that further asbestos exposure could be deadly. His chances of developing mesothelioma were very high. He was advised that he should not return to the power station. However, his employers, with their heads in the Apartheid sand, would not grant an alternative workplace environment until many months later. I was enraged at how the inhuman grains of incompetence and negligence had impacted common-sense employment statutes.

Onward Christian soldiers

I was also an Occupational Health Nurse and went to war against his employers. We learned a lot about asbestosis and asbestos-related issues from that point on. We discovered how pathetically slow the compensation process was for sufferers and their dependents and how big corporates and organs of the government covered up for each other at the expense of the poor and voiceless. However, cutting through the Gordian knot[54] of the defensive municipal hierarchy would have thwarted Alexander the Great and stumped Gordian (the father

---

[54] The term "Gordian knot," is commonly used to describe a complex or unsolvable problem. Shakespeare in Henry V refers to untying the Gordian Know tying up politics See https://www.history.com/news/what-was-the-gordian-knot

of King Midas). So we conducted our research and contacted foot soldiers to address this injustice.

We learned about rural mine dumps and mining towns where women were getting sick with asbestosis from washing the overalls of their menfolk who worked in those mines and industries. Many would die in squalor without their cases ever being heard. Sadly, so many years later, they still do. Large enterprises and mining corporations around our country are owned by foreigners. Now, some local financial giants call the tune – not humanity. The level of injustice and non-disclosure protectionism astounded us. Yes, we, the people of South Africa's soil, were viewed as dispensable to the Grand Apartheid dream – the son and daughters of Ham. As hewers of wood, we served only to fatten the bank balances of the influential oligarchs and autocrats. Still, today, the elite callously disregard the grassroots employees as expendable pawns in their callous game of economic chess.

Doctors in-the-know

Nevertheless, we found activist doctors who knew first-hand about the challenges and were fighting this injustice, and we teamed up with them. This eventually led to an almighty and drawn-out confrontation with Charles' municipal employers. Media coverage caused the guilty to cringe. During this time, Charles' medical file disappeared in transit to the responsible body in Pretoria - our nation's governance capital. Fortuitously, however, during one of my enraged states (righteous anger?) I had made copies of every document, including his X-Rays. When we heard about the missing file, we drove 1,500 km to Pretoria. Unannounced, we placed the copied file on the desk of a very awkward official. Houdini could not have done better with his hat and rabbit.

At last

Consequently, screening processes are now outsourced to professional experts in this field, and the process has changed for the better. However, caring for affected persons and their families remains a considerable challenge in the new Rainbow Nation - South Africa. Many voiceless families are abandoned to dire poverty and distress without compensation and support after loved ones die. We must still get to that pot of gold at the South African rainbow's end.

Charles has gone for screening annually for the last twenty-five years. He has spoken at the funerals of many of his colleagues who have succumbed to asbestosis. Charles got up from the table to order coffee at one of our Thursday Bible discussions and accountability meals with former offenders at a shopping mall. He and another man passed each other. The passerby was one of the doctors who had been part of the early stage of his diagnosis. As he spun around, the doctor shouted, "Charles?" Then came his incredulous, "Are you still alive?!" We all had a good laugh, and, looking back, our dear Lord had proved that He would lead us through the fire to victory.

The knot we tied was tested and secure

Our ministry began to take shape and grow. In parallel, our unique and loveable girls (Robyn and Lisa) and their step-brother, Rico (our precious adopted son), blossomed. Each will leave their footprints in this narrative. Lisa and Rico will also appear in subsequent chapters. So, hold tightly to your book as the turbulence of events in Lisa's chapter unfolds. Be prepared for the unexpected when Rico arrives!

Like my parents' marriage twenty-six years earlier, Charles and I also endured troubling times. Every dream faced the Apartheid-drawn question mark. For example, as the violence of the Apartheid tsunami swept across the country, a foreboding message from a visiting British Prime Minister, Harold MacMillan[55], rippled across the benches in the House of Parliament.

> The wind of change is blowing through this continent. Whether we like it or not, this growth of national consciousness is a political fact. I hope you won't mind my saying frankly that there are some aspects of your policies which make it impossible for us to do this without being false to our own deep convictions about the political destinies of free men to which in our own territories we are trying to give effect.

The South African government listened (with anger) to his words but did not heed MacMillan's winds of change warning. The Boers had, after all, gained ascendancy using weapons. The laagers had protected the Voortrekkers, and the army and air force were on call. That was the mindset of government leaders then.

---

55 Speech by the British Prime Minister Harold Macmillan to the Parliament of South Africa on 3 February 1960 in Cape Town. Macmillan, educated at Eton and a graduate of Baliol College (Oxford University) served in WW I and WW II) was known as "Supermac". His liberal sympathies rankled the grandees of the Conservative Party but he became Prime Minister from 1957 until his resignation in 1963. He died in 1986.

The next chapter records some humorous family secrets, a poem by young Robyn and our family's venture into the cruel world of HIV/AIDS, followed by Lisa's pre-school years and our visit to the islands of Zorba the Greek and an unforgettable flight home. The pages will allow readers to see the imprint of my God's grace and how the blessing of humour lightened our load.

Chapter Six

Robyn and Stevie Wonder

Charles and I had decided against starting our family immediately. However, Robyn was born nine months after our wedding, just as Stevie Wonder released his hit song, "Isn't she lovely!" Charles would sing that to her with stars in his eyes. We joked that we were grateful that she was born full term because many people used to calculate the forty weeks gestation period back then. We did not wish to initiate a scandal. Readers may remember that we had spent the night on Table Mountain while unmarried. Well, some might have wondered whether ours was a shotgun wedding!

Charles and I became proud parents during these desperate times when the milk of human kindness had generally soured. Rancid legislation was a magpie's-nest of virulent nationalism that spawned the lie of the dodgy, irrational, "separate but equal development" branding to mask the impacts of the destructive Apartheid tsunami.

Just before Christmas of 1976, cute baby Robyn bounced into our lives.

Robyn, a chip off two older blocks

Robyn was strong-willed (an undoubted family trait) and compassionate throughout her teens. She understood justice. A poem she wrote in the troubled days leading up to our first democratic election in South Africa in 1994 illustrates her innate sense of justice.

We lived in this politically volatile country we called home throughout Robyn's schooling years. Youth uprisings and violent protests, and killings were frequent across the country. Violence was met with violence. Many young people across the country lost their lives. I was sometimes convinced I would never see my beautiful daughter live to adulthood. Many times, I was crippled with an over-protective spirit. I had to protect her at all costs. Later she hated it, I think. How could a mother help her child understand genuine fears back then?

Robyn, schooling and Charles' new dentures

Charles and I sacrificed to place Robyn in a private school because we thought she would be safer from the police and uprisings. However, I hated that she had to be accepted through a quota system. Nevertheless, I reasoned that the decision was worth her life and conducive to her future career plans. We wanted her to learn and live. Our government-segregated coloured schools were explosive places. I refused to let her travel to school by public transport like her friends because I was scared she would be caught in a sudden flare-up of political unrest. I had seen many hurt children and others killed in the furore of civil unrest and anti-social behaviour. So, we took her to school every day of her school life - and fetched her. She was safe. Was I irrational? In hindsight, maybe so. But fear of what

I was witnessing around me compelled me. Indeed, other parents took the same protective measures. We tried to keep her life filled with positive experiences. We encouraged her interest in music, to explore the world and know that the South African Apartheid tsunami was not the norm.

The Trojan Horse

Robyn turned nine years old in December 1985. We could not envision a democratic and free South Africa in our lifetime. Ill will, mistrust and tension between people and groups were unmistakable.

15 October 1985 was a day when more demons from hell broke loose. Young people had gathered at nearby Thornton Road to protest the Apartheid government. Unbeknownst, the notorious riot squad had teamed up with the Railway Police to squash the rally.

A South African Railways truck with heavily armed security forces hidden behind wooden crates opened fire on youthful protestors immediately after their first stones hit the police vehicle. Three people (between eleven and twenty-one years) died in that barrage of gunfire. Many others were injured as security police chased after the protesters who sought refuge in nearby houses.

In 1988 a magistrate ruled that the Police had acted unreasonably. Thirteen Security Police were charged, and the case was referred to the Attorney General of the Cape, who refused to prosecute the men. A private prosecution by families of the deceased ended in their complete acquittal. Those fracture lines still run deep in our national psyche.

A LEGACY OF SENSES

My mind I leave, that you may understand
The fury and rage born of Apartheid's hand.
Eyes I give that you may see past fear, confusion, and misery,
The rising sun with glowing rays of hope and promise of better days.
Ears I leave, oh, hear the cries
From dusty, bleeding townships long hidden from your eyes.
Nose to smell, not burning barricades nor stench of death,
But fragrance ascending in pleasing breath.
Mouth to speak words true and wise,
"Hush, deceiving voices, no more lies!"
Arms to embrace, not push away
Those who hurt in our land today.
Hands I leave, with tender touch,
Bind wounds, heal scars, and SERVE
Where years of injustice have stolen so much.
Feet, to step from comforts warm
Into shoes of lives so beaten and worn.
My spirit, God-given, I give in return.
Of love for one's brother, hard lesson to learn.
My heart sends out its pulse of life,
As it pleads,
"Sweet land, cease bitter strife."

Robyn Kadalie

Out of the mouth of babes

Robyn understood South Africa's dual world. She rubbed shoulders with the super-rich and the extremely poor. One day she was due to go home with one of her private school friends. The chauffeur came to pick them up at school in a Rolls Royce. Robyn was too embarrassed to be seen in it; she shrunk into the seat.

By contrast, at the end of her first year at this great private school, the Grade 1 class had to write a letter to Santa, asking him to bring a Christmas gift for their dad. The parents were invited to view these letters at a year-end function. Well, Charles and I walked around the room admiring the fancy requests to Santa for the other dads. From golf sets to fancy new cars. We got to Robyn's letter - she asked Santa to please bring her dad new underpants and a pair of socks! Indeed, I was tired of patching socks, as my dad had taught me. So, she had a point. Those power station safety boots chewed his socks like a dog gnawing a bone. For a long time, I wondered what the other parents thought.

A dental event

We shared laughs over silly things, usually at the most inappropriate times. For example, while sitting in the front row of a church where Charles was the guest preacher. A congregation member stood up and asked for prayer for her son, who had been stabbed. She said the doctor had told her they could not do anything for her son. He would probably be a "vegetarian" for the rest of his life! That malapropism triggered the worst laughing fit imaginable – in the front row! Charles had just fitted new dentures, and we waited on the edge of our seats for them to pop out of his mouth with the first "Phu" syllable. Charles, who is always on cue, did not disappoint us – his new teeth all but completely plopped out - the rest is history.

Robyn, determination, and Henry Heimlich

Robyn was headstrong from her earliest years. You know what they say about the terrible twos. She ran away from home before she was three years old. I had rapped her one (not with a plate across her head), and she was so offended that she stopped crying and climbed through a window when I was busy in the kitchen. She went to look for her daddy to complain. She knew the church met at a children's home and was heading there. A security guard at a shop two blocks away recognised her and brought her home.

When Robyn was in her third year, she choked on one of my favourite sweets - round sweet balls. She went blue and could not breathe. I did a Heimlich manoeuvre on her and turned her upside down, dislodging the sweet, and, while pacifying her, shouted, "do not ever eat one of those sweets again! You will die"! Now I understand what the words "irony and paradox" mean! I put the tin out of reach. A few minutes later, she came crying and slamming her little fists together, screaming, "I want to die, I want to die"! Mind you, those sweets were rather good. I can still visualize the tin!

A burglar foiled

There was a knock on our door, Lisa was a baby, and Robyn was not yet five. Charles and I were both at work. The workman told our home help (who was living with us) that the house owner (he had forgotten his name) had booked him to come and repair the house alarm. So Serita let him in. She had Lisa on her arm, and he asked her to help him stretch the cable he needed to use. He positioned her holding the cable tightly in the backyard and fed it through the kitchen window. Robyn followed the uncle around inquisitively, so he asked her to help him. He asked her to hold the other end of the cable in her room and to pull tightly. She and Serita held it taught, not realising who was at the other end. While the burglar was clearing out the cupboards in our bedroom, Robyn thought it was strange that he was not coming back again. She cleverly jammed the end of the cable in her toy box lid and went to find Serita and Lisa. She discovered that she and Serita were pulling on the ends of the same cable. Now Serita was a big, tall lady. She stormed into the house, and with her shouting, the burglar fled through the window, leaving the stacked-up bags behind. He also left a roll of cable that Charles used for his private electrical work for a long time. That was the only burglar that had left us something valuable and of use.

Robyn opens her heart to AIDS victims

Robyn was fifteen years old when the first child with AIDS came to live with us. A small procession followed in the ensuing years. She and her sister loved a little AIDS orphan back to life. He was crippled by the disease and was estimated not to live beyond six weeks. Today he is their irrepressible 30-year-old brother by adoption. Rico is healed of HIV/AIDS.

When she was barely out of her teens, Robyn's compassion was purified by fire again. One of our little AIDS orphans became extremely ill when Charles and I were overseas. She comforted him in the hospital and sat beside him while he died. He was fourteen months old.

HIV/AIDS – stories from my files

While working in a specialised Aged Care set-up, I was asked to write a chapter in a book. The text was to be supported by photographs of the struggles of growing old and being poor in South Africa. I wrote the chapter on the impact of HIV/AIDS on the elderly poor. With credit to the publishers[56], I include relevant extracts from this chapter in my story because the content is an essential part of my life and learning. These are the real faces behind the statistics. More than learning from them, they touched our family life and emotions in immeasurable ways. These were our precious and much-loved foster children.

My name is Sonwabile

"My name means, Happiness. I am fourteen months old. I will not die as a nameless, faceless HIV/AIDS statistic. I will die loved. Though abused and abandoned, I will feel my heartbeat against yours. Though my infant lips will never mouth the words of question and insight I yearn to speak, my heart will talk to you through my pain-filled smile and tired eyes. Though coughing rips my lungs apart until it seems the next breath will be denied, I feel and taste your comforting tears mingling with mine, and I know you share my pain and love me as your own. My gaze, now unfocussed, will see your compassionate eyes, warm heart and hand that lovingly connects me to God. And as I prepare to wing my journey homeward, know this - my name is Happiness - anguish, like a living thing, clutches my foster siblings too."

---

[56] Faces of Age Published: Kraal Publishers, Brandfort, 2005 Edition: First Edition

Jason

"Jason had just turned four when he was diagnosed HIV positive. Ignorance and irrational fear forced him to live, sleep and eat with family dogs for four months. Physically beaten, emotionally broken, and with trust shattered, he existed. How much he had lived in so short a life. But he learned to laugh again. For a little while."

Magrieta

"Magrieta lived with her grandmother in a squatter camp. Just turned nine, two drunken family friends raped her. The confusion and intense emotion of puberty and adolescence paled into insignificance in the wake of the rapists' attacks and the malicious virus that had become part of her life. She died of full-blown AIDS a week before her 16th birthday."

Rico

"Rico knew abandonment, deprivation, disability, and disease from birth. He flew into our homes and hearts like a bird with a broken wing. Orphaned by AIDS, severely infected with HIV, crippled by Polio, and riddled with miliary TB and fetal alcohol damage, he was given six weeks to live. Yet, Rico was ordained amongst the blessed. We saw our God demonstrate His healing power. In the absence of ARV medication in those early years, Rico seroconverted to HIV negative at eighteen months. Today, he is our irrepressible thirty-year-old adopted son. He received some medication for miliary TB while in the hospital, but there was no medication for HIV/AIDS. He was discharged to our care without any medication. Just palliative care because they thought he would die!"

Robyn and our youngest daughter Lisa shared their parents and home with many other children. Our girls witnessed and helped them through pain and suffering. They have learned from each one, just as Charles and I have – they are richer in spirit and understanding.

Lisa, the achiever

Lisa was born four and a half years after Robyn's perfectly executed normal birth with a midwife in attendance. We had no medical aid then.

However, medical aid was on tap when Lisa came along. Charles and I opted to go to an upmarket, fancy, titled obstetrician who would witness the birth. We were so excited about that. However, the doctor misread my gestation period and induced me six weeks prematurely. The student monitoring my contractions did not recognize the signs of distress in my unborn baby. Being a trained midwife, I kept my eyes on the monitors and realised something was seriously amiss. Each time I had a contraction, the fetal heart seemed to stop. I explained to the student the urgency of getting help.

The obstetrician was delayed in attending to Lisa and me. The situation spiralled into a life-threatening condition for my unborn baby and me. Lisa went into transverse arrest with a shoulder presentation. In an emergency caesarian section, she had to be pulled up the birth canal again, sustaining a greenstick fracture of her newborn femur. I heard her cry when I woke up and knew something was amiss. The doctors closed ranks and did not answer my queries. I heard whispers about "the midwife whose little knowledge was dangerous." Charles could not witness the birth as we had planned. However, he was present at the birth of our second grandchild Kyla when Robyn invited us to be with her during the birth process. That was incredibly special.

The post-birth narrative

I had just started working full-time for the Cape Town City Mission's aged care division, and my four-month-old new arrival could come to my workplace with me. The older residents and Aunty Ethel mothered her. However, Lisa's expected developmental milestones were unachievable.

Pre-School Education – negative and positive experiences and creativity

Lisa had intense separation anxiety that interfered with her ability to attend preschool. However, her teacher would put her out of the class and abandon her to cry. The teacher could not manage the crying of a four-year-old child and never contacted me. One day the Principal called Charles and me to a meeting in her office. She told us that Lisa was a potential delinquent! Oh my! We were grilled about our marriage and relationship, insisting that we hid something that caused Lisa's crying and anxiety. They could not take her back and gave us a psychologist's details.

Undaunted, we found an outstanding preschool, La Petite. The Principal agreed to give Lisa a chance. The open door led to Lisa being loved and nurtured by competent and empathetic professionals. Furthermore, they believed in us. One day the principal called me, saying, "stop what you're doing! We got Lisa into the pool! She is swimming on her own. You've got to come and see this!" I dropped everything and jumped into my car. Then I stood at a window where she could not see me and watched her in awe. That display and growth were just exhilarating to observe. By the way, Lisa is no delinquent. Charles and I remain happily married.

Moving forwards, we had to think of her future, post-La Petite. Was Lisa on the autistic spectrum? Did she have cerebral palsy? Signs and developmental delays pointed to this, but no one in the medical team would talk to me about it. I knew she would drown in a regular class with 30 - 40 children ready to start primary school. But I could not get her into a classified school for children with special needs. The rule was that a child had to fail Sub A (Gr 1) three successive years before qualifying for admission. I still ponder what bright mind had devised such an illogical rule. I came close to swearing. I still wonder whether the chicken or the egg came first!

I eventually got an appointment at a clinic in London (UK). With that report, I could enrol her into Eros School for Cerebral Palsied Children in Cape Town, and she could complete her schooling there on a practical level.

Watching her go to her finishing school dance and dinner at the end of that school year was magic. They confirmed that she had mild cerebral palsy, general muscle tone weakness on her right side, perceptual imbalances, and an Autistic Spectrum Disorder. We noticed that she had a reduced pain threshold, and to this day, we watch the bath water temperatures and regulate hot drinks because she scalds herself. For example, she had not felt a large boil on one occasion until it was ready to rupture.

Lisa has unique gifts. She loves colours and can be spontaneously and outrageously funny - and stubborn beyond measure (probably a genetic link to her mom – not stubborn - but determined). You cannot sway her if her mind tells her not to do something.

Lisa and our travels around the Greek islands (with apologies to Zorba the Greek)

When Lisa was nearly four, and Robyn was nine, we travelled to Israel and the Greek islands. She turned four on the island of Mykonos. We arrived in the evening and checked in at our pensione. Lisa would not settle because it was her birthday, and we had promised that she would have a birthday cake when we arrived. So, we dumped our bags and went out looking for a cake. However no one had a birthday cake, but we found a sizeable muffin-like thing, took it back and got ready to sing Happy Birthday. But no, Lisa wanted birthday candles on her cake. We went out again to look for birthday candles, but no one had even heard of such things. Finally, one café owner told us to go into a church and take four candles from the altar. Can you picture us sneaking into this church and taking four long, thin candles from the altar? They looked so incongruous on that big muffin that even my God would giggle. Lisa was happy, and we could sleep. I hope Charles left money on the altar to pay for the candles.

On the island of Paros, Lisa decided that she had walked enough and was not taking another step. Charles was tired of carrying her, so we told her we would leave and walk on if she did not wish to follow us. Lisa planted her feet on the cobbled street, crossed her arms and watched us move off. She just stood there. Well, happily, our God came to our rescue when we arrived at our pensione. We walked up to the flat rooftop to see the view of the street, and there it was! A rusty old pushcart.

The owner had forgotten about it and had no problem with Charles fixing it up to get the wheels turning. Lisa was a happy tourist from that point. Well, if Robyn could ride in a Rolls Royce while hiding in the back seat, Lisa could be proudly wheeled around in a cart chauffeured by her ever-caring and patient father!

Creativity wins the flight

As the holiday in Paros ended, we set out to board a small plane from Paros to Athens. The flight was delayed, and our bags had been checked in. We could not take anything in the cabin because of the size of the plane. Then horror of horrors, Lisa did not get to the toilet in time and wet herself. She wanted clean pants. But there was none to be had – they were neatly packed in the luggage in the aeroplane. Nothing we could say or do would alter her understanding of our situation. We were finally getting ready to board, but Lisa's pants were wet, and she wanted a dry pair. The attendants were rushing us on, and we would delay boarding. However, Lisa wanted dry pants. Consequently, Robyn was unhappy flying from Paros to Athens without panties, but that was all we could do. It is still a family joke.

Lisa's lesson about birth

Readers may recall that Robyn had a normal birth, while Lisa was born by cesarean section. After our trip, sitting around the dining room table with a guest, the crockery and cutlery were laid out like Thelma would have liked. Everybody (including Charles) was on their best behaviour. However, Robyn kept baiting Lisa during dinner. Her sister would not back down. Then the last straw broke the camel's back as Robyn's teasing continued. Lisa turned her head and glared at Robyn – her eyes were like pools of bubbling lava. She was incandescent with anger as she spat out, "YOU! I come out of Mommy's stomach, but you come out of Mommy's bum!".

Well, back to normality. We enjoyed our meal flavoured with howls of laughter and much cleaning up of chewed vegetables splashed across the table. For once, Robyn had no answer – she remained schtum! Thelma would have objected to the loss of formal decorum, and dad would have rolled on the floor with laughter.

We had returned to the land of our birth and into a bitterly divided country. The younger generation had begun to act out their pent-up feelings, and Charles and I had to face a new swelling surge of tsunamis. While in Israel, we watched the unedited news about South Africa with interest and growing alarm.

The narrative continues in Chapter 7, where readers will meet our respectable Mr Christian. We will discover the Prophet's Chamber, learn about smelling danger, understand my God's thread of protection, and discipling amongst the aged and murder on four wheels. Readers will also read about Charles' bodyguard. This rainbow guaranteed the fulfilment of a vision, a pertinent reminder of Noah's experience, and a justifiable demand for equality.

Chapter Seven

Facing lessons about loss, my God, danger and the other Tsunamis

Early in our marriage Charles and I learned not to place too much value on earthly possessions. Material things could be instantly lost. We knew, too, that the world was not overflowing with people who were the salt of the earth. Such kind and beautiful individuals were in great demand.

So, we saved as hard as possible and finally had enough to place a deposit, secure a plot, and build a home on a new parcel of land in a "safe" area. We were excited. I still have the architect's plans for the house.

Oops!

Mr Christian was well up with Christian lingo and impressed Charles and me. His home help was a resolute Christian believer whom we happened to know. Mr Christian could be the builder of our house. Because my father was a master bricklayer craftsman who knew a thing or two about buildings (and builders) and had been around the block many times, we arranged a meeting with Mr Christian. My father was unimpressed with the tone and professional approach of the meeting. However, against his wise advice, we handed Mr Christian our savings; that was the last we saw of our dream, which turned into a nightmare. We were shattered. Our lease on our house was ending soon, and we had no plan B. We moved to a converted garage with no shower or ablution facilities. We had to go to the main house to use the toilet or shower. We lived there for about a year. However, we made ourselves comfortable, overcame our anger and indignation, and learned about humility. After all, the baby Jesus was born in a less-than-normal setting.

We started to see the funny side of our naiveté, and then our God stepped in. Charles was qualified by now and working in a power station. The municipality was subdividing a tract of land for housing in a part of the Cape Flats where (we) Coloured people could own land. As a staff member, Charles could bid on a piece of land without a deposit (we had none in any event). His successful bid led to our elation that knew no bounds. Many faith adventures would fill our years in that house. Ah, trust in our God was not in vain.

The Prophet's Chamber

In 1979 when Robyn was two years old, we moved into the first home we called our own. It was a little house on a newly subdivided land where we Coloured people could own property. We had no road, garage, boundary walls and no immediate neighbours.

Soon our closest neighbours would comprise young families starting out, and they moved in within a few months of each other. Landlines and a binding community spirit characterised our environment. The emergency numbers on their fridges started with "Uncle Charlie", then the police! Many hair-raising and hilarious adventures arose from those "Uncle Charlie" calls. Charles had a pickaxe handle as a weapon – he had never enrolled at a martial arts dojo or even handled a foil in a fencing class. He had a firearm competency certificate because of his power station responsibilities and the fact that it was a national key point. Still, he was never granted a licence by the police authorities because of his skin colour. However, whoever was at the receiving end of his pickaxe handle knew he had done something wrong that threatened the lives and safety of the families around us. We could not wait for the police in those years. We would be dead by the time they arrived.

We committed our home to be a healing space for those in need (we were, after all, in a "safe" area). My God had impressed the story of the woman of Shunem on my heart[57]. That is what I wanted, so that is what we did. The most amazing people entered our home, and the Prophet's Chamber remains an inviting oasis for hurting and broken people. Little did we know that uninvited visitors would also arrive in our "safe" area.

The smell of danger

Our Little House on the Prairie launched as a stand-alone on an open field in a "safe" area. Having taken occupation six weeks earlier, we prepared for our first Easter in our home. The window putty was still soft.

I had worked many shifts in the trauma unit at my first training hospital. The smell of dried, bloodied, and dirty clothes had

---

[57] 2 Kings 4 describes her home as where Elisha was given rest and hospitality whenever he passed through the town. She built a room for him with the basic things he would need to be comfortable when he needed rest and a meal.

never left my nostrils. That distinct odour woke me up at 0300 that Easter Sunday morning. I opened my eyes and made out the shapes of three strange men around our bed. I called Charles's name, and as he woke, he was pinned to his pillow with a machete to his neck. We knew we were in deep trouble. However, our God, our tsunami whisperer, was with us – we could trust him. Apparently, our calmness disturbed the three men. One was highly agitated and encouraged the others to "finish him [Charles] off." We watched in complete quietness of spirit as they stripped us of everything of any value in our room, including his wedding suit. At the same time, they continued to threaten us and said they would shoot Charles if he moved.

While Robyn lay between us, sleeping restfully, our uninvited visitors told us they had been in our house for over two hours. I must have fetched Robyn from her room while they were inside. However, our God had kept Charles sleeping, but not me. The pickaxe handle would have cost Charles his life if they had woken him.

The contents from the front of our Little House on the Prairie had been loaded into our car. One of the men told us they had escaped from prison and were hungry. They wanted to know where the food was. Well, it was Easter, and like traditional coloured people, we had more than enough pickled fish and hot cross buns stored away. I spontaneously told them where to find the

prepared meal in the kitchen. In the dark, because they had switched off the main electricity supply, I asked, "Can I make you all some hot coffee?" Charles punched me in the ribs. However, I thought that if I could just get them seated around my kitchen table, I could listen to their stories and speak life to them. That was and is still the core purpose of my kitchen table. Sadly, I never had that chat because the offer of coffee depended on them restoring the current to boil the water.

Locating the culprits and a thread from the past

When fingerprints were lifted, the police confirmed that these men were highly dangerous, had escaped from detention and were wanted for armed robberies, murder and rape. The police commander said when we told him we had not been harmed, "It's only God that protected you."

The thread

Amazingly, another tapestry thread of God's plan prepared us for this scene. The detective assigned to our case had become a first-time father on the day Robyn was born. His wife and I lay in labour next to each other in the same ward. He took the issue personally. A newspaper report a few weeks later read, "Police bullet ends a life of crime." The murder and robbery squad had staked out a den where the man who had pinned Charles down with a machete while asking for prayer was shot dead. He and his two mates had killed a man with a broken bottleneck. The other two went to prison for a long time.

Ironically, I oversaw the local community health clinic in the same troubled community where these men lived and operated. Anonymously, I looked after the deceased man's baby-feeding needs for the next year of his life. With hindsight,

Charles and I realised that by learning about empathy in the hospital for the mentally ill our God was preparing us for a future ministry role with prisoners. We could empathise (in measure) with their pain, anger, hate and violence.

Helping the seniors

However, we also knew we were to care for senior citizens. For the next twenty-five years, we served in this field. The man who introduced me to my faith adventure gave me the responsibility and the opportunity to develop the Aged Care Department for the Cape Town City Mission. The first residential home for the elderly poor in that community opened on 10 May 1982. Bruce Duncan was central to that process. Community care for the physically and mentally weakened older persons was sorely lacking for those classified as "other than white" by Apartheid's legislature. There were no rehabilitative services in our communities. Consequently, the dream of a purpose-built community facility never faded. In one discussion about this, Bruce told me to put my thoughts, my dream, on paper. Two weeks later, I took my written plan to him. He said, "I already have a model for this!" He scrummaged in a cupboard and, from the recesses, pulled out a model that closely paralleled the purpose and spaces I had written down. The plan included the indoor therapy pool with a wheelchair ramp! Coincidence? I think not. This was another thread of the tapestry my God had woven for Charles and me. The astonishing detail would emerge many years later when I managed the GH Starck Centre.

A haven in the face of Apartheid's turbulent political tsunami[58]

By mid-1980, South Africa was in flames. Growing acts of violent resistance and uprisings met with even more brutal responses from the security police and state defence forces. The government declared a partial emergency on 20 July 1985 across 83 districts. In Cape Town, our townships were like war zones. The security police - known as the riot squad, were ruthless. They had orders to curb the onslaughts of the outcomes of a 400 years-old politically-empowered divisive culture that gave birth to the Apartheid tsunami. Ironically, the Bible that the creators of Apartheid thought sanctioned their hideous racist philosophy also taught that what is sown will be reaped[59].

One night, we had been warned by families we knew to stay away from the area we worked in because of the persistent, violent unrest and clashes with riot police. Riot police vehicles, called Casspirs, brought indiscriminate death, pain and fear. Regardless, Charles decided he would attend a prayer meeting and support families we knew living in fear.

Murder on wheels

On his way home that night, driving through the mayhem, he saw Bruce Duncan running towards the Cape Town City Mission children's home. His face was wrapped in a towel because of the tear gas all around him. Charles stopped hurriedly and loaded Bruce into his car so they could collect his station wagon. Bruce hastily described how a young man on his way home after work was shot while standing next to him by

---

[58] The term "tsunami" comes from the Japanese 津波, meaning "harbour wave."
[59] Galatians 6:7.

someone in a car careering across the road. Bruce and community members had managed to get the young man's limp body into a house. In the kitchen, with Bruce cradling his head and wiping his brow, the victim opened his eyes, gasped, and died. Despite his tears, Bruce wanted to get the body out of the house before the police arrived. This young man was proof that the so-called upholders of law and order were using live ammunition to disperse crowds. Of course, they always gave the assurance that they only used rubber bullets and tear gas.

So, Charles and Bruce swapped vehicles. With Bruce driving, they returned to the house. Charles hurriedly lowered the back seat of the station wagon.

The police had received word of where the body was and arrived at the house just after Charles and Bruce left. Before the police had kicked down the front door to gain entry, Bruce, Charles and other community men had carried the body out of the back door. They loaded the slain young man into the back of the waiting station wagon parked in a back lane and sped off to the GH Starck Centre for the Aged, which I was managing.

Bruce then contacted the activist lawyers to witness this tragedy of a young life cut short while standing beside him. After the lawyers had taken photos of the victim and the bullet hole in his chest, and Bruce had given his eyewitness statement, he called the ambulance. When escorting the ambulance men carrying the body bag, he saw the untidy pile of many bodies in the ambulance. Each corpse was a victim of the stealthy, unjust and hideous Apartheid tsunami that had begun to gestate across the southern tip of South Africa in 1652.

The young man was Paul. He was the grandson of Ma Ruthie, one of the elderly mothers who had been evicted from District 6. Her home had been one of the Cape Town City Mission's regular meeting places for the spiritual support of the families around her. Charles had to tell Ma Ruthie about her grandson's death that night. A week later, Charles and Bruce headed the funeral cortege on foot down Voortrekker Road[60] (oh, the irony of fate!). The Casspirs and army trucks soon sidled up close to the funeral cortege, and the comments from some of the security forces were far from complimentary. Charles and Bruce looked straight ahead and eventually officiated at the graveside – another innocent young man laid to rest – dust to dust but forever in the memories of others. Paul lies in the same graveyard where the founder of the Cape Town City Mission lies buried for 61 years.

In hindsight, I recall the young man was standing next to Bruce when the killers shot from their speeding vehicle. We still wonder if Bruce was the intended target. In the eyes of the "law", Bruce was marked as a political troublemaker – a "kaffir boetie"[61]. His outspoken and peaceful activism in opposition to Apartheid and support for Nelson Mandela was well known. He had his share of enemies and had been taken to the Philippi Police Station with a fellow activist, where he had to listen to a policeman reading Romans 13. At the same time, his bleeper

---

60 Many roads are named in tribute to the descendants of the settlers who came to the Cape and then, to seek their own slice of the country, had travelled to the northern parts of the country. They were called the Voortrekkers – the Boer pioneers who took part in the trek from the Cape Colony to the Transvaal in 1834–37.
61 The Afrikaans term Kaffir-boetie (Kaffir brother) – a derogatory term described a white person who fraternised with or sympathized with the justified grievances of the disenfranchised black community. White racists coined the term "negro lover "in English-speaking countries.

never stopped reminding him that his friends were standing by.

Nonetheless, in the middle of all this turbulence, Charles and I lived, worked and took our daughter to school - like countless others.

Saved by an angel

1990 saw the Apartheid tsunami increase ferocity as determined youth protesters took up the cudgels against injustice. A significant national stay away was called, and everything reached a standstill. However, our staff continued to come to work because of the needs of the frail in our care. Primrose was one of our cleaning staff. After work, she could not get a bus or taxi to go home to her family in Khayelitsha (22 km away from the GH Starck Centre). Charles told her to wait for him, went to the GH Starck Centre, swapped vehicles and left with Primrose.

Staff for the next shift heard that he had left with her and raised the alarm with me. All roads in and out of the township were "No Go" zones. Barricades were burning everywhere, the security police in their armoured vehicles sprayed bullets, and angry people built and protected barriers of wood and burning tyres. Protesters threw stones at the hated supporters of the Apartheid tsunami.

The staff mobilised to pray. There were no mobile phones yet, so there was no way I could contact Charles. We had to trust my God – the Apartheid tsunami whisperer.

Meanwhile, Charles had been ambushed and trapped at one of the main burning barricades off the highway. A 300-strong, angry, riotous mob had surrounded Primrose and Charles. The car door was ripped open, and the ignition keys were removed. The car was lifted up with him and Primrose inside while the mob raged. Petrol-filled cans were on hand to set the vehicle alight. Charles and Primrose were about to be listed among the latest casualties of the Dutch East India's avaricious impact on our country. Suddenly from amongst that loud and angry mob, a voice rang out, loud and clear. "Discipline!" The car was dropped on its wheels. The man with a powerful voice stood at the car door. He was dressed in the banned Umkhonto we Sizwe uniform[62]. He asked Charles a barrage of quick questions and then told him to drive off and, if he came through the barricade, he would be allowed through the others. "But I can't", Charles told him.

"Why not?" this man with authority in his voice asked.

"Because someone took my ignition keys," Charles replied.

The man disappeared into the swelling crowd. Within two minutes, he came back with the car keys. How was that possible? He told Charles to drive off, but Charles said he would not go unless the man got in the car with him.

They took Primrose safely home, but Charles now had to return the way he came, so he insisted that the man get him past the barricade again. The uniformed freedom fighter told Charles to slow down as they passed the burning barricade – a wall of fire. He opened the door, slipped out of the moving car, and disappeared down an embankment. Charles made it home,

---

[62] The military wing of the then-banned African National Congress.

white as a sheet and in shock. He could not move from the car at first. I did not even know he was outside.

To this day, we believe that the man with authority in his voice, dressed in the banned MK uniform, was an angel sent by our God, the tsunami whisperer.

Another thread

The GH Starck Centre epitomised all aspects of geriatric care, from residential, terminal, and dementia care to managing community ageing. Our facilities were known for innovation and best practices, and the team and I received national and international awards. We saw my God release miracle after miracle as our most fantastic team lived and worked to make a dream come true. For six years, a group of older women met every workday to pray that my God would release funding. We needed to establish and build a purpose-built facility for the elderly poor, stroke survivors, and those suffering from dementia on the vacant plot across the road from the GH Starck Centre. Do you remember the plans Bruce extracted from a cupboard many years previously?

We also needed a suitable van to transport stroke-affected persons to our centre for therapeutic activities. We had no money, but I had a picture of what we needed on my prayer board! Well, my God spoke to a lady called Chris through my friend Audrey in the USA, and she sold some shares to assist us with the vehicle funds. The foreign exchange conversion equated to the amount on the quote. Was this another coincidence? I know it was my God!

Concept drawings for the new Aged Care Centre and an architect's model injected fervour into our prayer for the next ten years.

Stand aside Noah

We did not have any money to begin the project. Still, one evening dashing from my office to the car in the falling rain, a double rainbow of a promise dipped right down in the centre of the field where the building  was to be. It took my breath away. I dashed inside, shouting to staff nearby to run to the rainbow. I found my camera and just snapped away. There were no smartphones then. The team and I just knew it would happen. We would see a dream fulfilled. We had no idea when - but it would happen. Rehoboth Age Exchange was on the way.

Affirmative action

One major potential funder suggested that the plans were too elaborate for a community like Hanover Park. The sub-economic "suburb" spawned in the wake of removing people of colour from the hub of Cape Town life was not a good investment. Hanover Park existed because of the uninvited 1652 mindset that had evicted over 60,000 people from their homes and dumped them in a sand-swept township because of their skin colour[63]. However, I told the funder we wanted the same quality we would expect in the more affluent suburbs[64]. I was not interested in perpetuating a discriminatory pattern that allowed some to have better provisions than others. I would not perpetuate an inherited "parallel but unequal development" concept. Subsequently, we received more than twice the initial amount offered.

Along with the incredible support of three other funders, the Rehoboth Age Exchange opened its doors in July 2002. Fully funded and equipped by R15 million. My God had added thread after thread to His tapestry. It was time to uproot and begin a new ministry opening for us.

Chapter 8 leads us through the valley of the shadow of death and destruction. Readers will see how my God, who moves mysteriously, ensured that the damage of numerous tsunamis never swamped my place on the Rock of Ages. My life was a predestined journey of riding the turbulent waves – and emerging triumphantly on the other side.

---

[63] To understand the context of this evil act, please access South African History Online at https://www.sahistory.org.za/article/cape-town-segregated-city.
[64] The diplomatic language covered the use of the "them and us" – the inheritance from 1652 and 1820 where the colonising settlers came to bring civilisation to the "savages".

Chapter Eight

Overcoming Tsunamis while on My Heavenly Father's Lap

On 14 May 2015, I went into the hospital for a routine carpal tunnel release on both wrists. The surgeon was one of the most respected hand surgeons in Cape Town. By the time I was discharged later that day, I did not notice anything substantially wrong other than twinges of post-operative pain. By the next day, the discomfort was much worse. Several young people came to our home to be baptized that afternoon. I was making a large pot of soup with one hand. The swelling in my right-hand fingers was severe, and the pain was almost unbearable. Charles took me to the emergency unit that evening, but they discharged me with anti-inflammatories and pain medication.

By the following day, I suspected that I had a significant infection. I was desperately sick. The little finger on my right hand had swollen to an unrecognizable size. In Cape Town townships, we have a cheap sausage called a Penny Polony (made from goodness knows what). My finger could have provided good marketing material for the sausage vendors.

On this occasion, the emergency staff member called the surgeon. A battery of blood tests and cultures were run. I had picked up an aggressive staphylococcus infection during surgery. I was in trouble. The infection was racing through my bloodstream. Over the next four days, I was in the operating theatre daily to have my pinkie and palm of my hand opened and flushed out to rid my tissues of the life-threatening bug. Numerous antibiotics were tried with no effect. Finally, one culture showed promise on the fifth day. The antibiotic started neutralising the bug that had nearly taken my life. Over the next three months, many occupational therapy treatments restored some function to my hand, but my finger remains deformed.

Precisely four months later - oblivion

The Olifants River meanders through the breathtakingly beautiful Cederberg mountains of the Western Cape. Charles and I had been camping with six young adult men we had mentored over time. Each had had a past tagged with criminal behaviour, drug misuse and alienation from family, society and the church.

They had no character references acceptable to the world of commerce and industry; education was one irritant from their pock-marked past. Indeed, each epitomised those to whom the founder of the Cape Town City Mission had ministered.

Each had become one of our spiritual sons. They had come to know the One who had mastered their tsunamis. Charles and I had witnessed the miracle of how their transforming lives had impacted their communities. They began to take others by the hand and lead them to freedom.

Some of our special friends had accompanied us to help prepare meals for a few days. 14 September 2015 was such a day. It started beautifully as we ended a perfect weekend.

The weaving of the tapestry

The surge of the unexpected tsunami hit hard, and my neatly planned little garden was about to be ploughed up. It was a strange day. Lisa (my youngest daughter) was unsettled. Her sandal strap broke, and she wanted it fixed. Charles took a cable tie and side cutters from the car I would drive. He made the sandal wearable and threw the side cutters into the van he was driving. We prayed for a safe journey home. Ah! The threads were coming together – again.

> Disturb us, Lord, to dare more boldly,
> To venture on wider seas
> Where storms will show your mastery;
> Where losing sight of land,
> We shall find the stars.
>
> Author Unknown

Because Charles had to deal with a business issue on our journey, we decided to change our route and explore Goedverwacht. This old Moravian mission town was the venue for his business meeting. Our campers had never been there.

We had a guided tour, met several inhabitants, and chatted while waiting for Charles.

As we were saying our goodbyes, the weather suddenly changed, and dark storm clouds hovered over the mountain around us. Peals of thunder echoed in the valley. Lightning zig-zagged across the sky, and one jagged bolt set a section of the mountain foliage alight. The sound and light show was followed by pelting rain. The mountain fire gave way to the deluge. Still, our tsunami was yet to morph into the juggernaut that smashed lives on the highway and catapulted me into oblivion – was this the route to look beyond the stars?

The crash

That is the last memory I have. I drove behind Charles. Two of our friends and helpers, Lisa and one of our young men, were travelling with me. The rest of the young men were in the van Charles was driving. We would be home in an hour.

Charles told me he saw the delivery van coming from the opposite direction. It passed him at blistering speed. He instinctively glanced in his rear-view mirror. He saw the impact in his mirror. He spun his car around. He did not expect anyone to be alive in the carnage.

Two of our helper friends and one of our young men were already dead. I was barely alive, my chest was crushed, and my leg was broken. I was trapped in the wreckage. I was choking with the seatbelt jammed in my neck, blood gushing from my head. Charles could not loosen the seatbelt. He thought Lisa was dead too. Then seeing her eyes flicker, called her name and asked if she was OK. She nodded, dazed but conscious and trapped in the back seat alongside her dead older friends slumped beside her.

> Disturb us, Lord, when
> We are too well pleased with ourselves,
> When our dreams have come true
>
> (Author Unknown)

The side cutters – an invaluable thread

The young men, traumatised by what they saw, told me how they heard Charles talk to our God and ask for my life. Suddenly, Charles remembered the side cutters used for Lisa's shoe repair (he had tossed them into his van). He cut me loose from the seatbelt, and the young men helped him ease my mangled body out of the wreck and stabilise my breathing. Then amid strewn wreckage, glass fragments, and motor oil, out of nowhere, a sparkling clean face cloth lay within his reach. He could staunch the bleeding from my head until the rescue vehicles arrived and took over.

Miraculously, Lisa was cut out of the wreckage without a scratch on her body and no broken bones. Her spectacles were crushed into her face. She was covered in glass from head to toe, but no marks were on her body. Lisa has always been afraid of hospitals. Many months later, she told me she thought she was watching me die. My 34-year-old autistic, intellectually challenged daughter began her nightmare because she could not process and express herself in therapeutic counselling. The aftershock would overtake her five years later.

My consciousness returned five days after the accident when the doctor with Charles gave me the dreaded news. I remember holding my breath as the doctor gently spoke. Had Lisa died too? My protective, maternal instincts soon abated - the doctor told me she would be OK. She had no physical injuries.

I heard I was seriously injured; my condition was critical and unstable, and recovery would be long and hard. However, an operation to fix the fracture and injuries to my leg was urgent because blood clots and infections might complicate my already crammed medical agenda. Consequently, the first of many significant reconstructive operations followed over the next three years.

> We ask You to push back
> The horizons of our hopes;
> And to push into the future
> In strength, courage, hope, and love.
>
> Source: Author Unknown

Painful lessons from this tsunami are woven into the tapestry

I learned a new definition of pain over the following three years. Every movement was excruciating. A friend told me later that I was so swollen that I occupied the whole hospital bed. The blood pressure cuff was attached to the only limb extremity they could use, my right ankle. I questioned my God every waking moment about why I lived while four people died. Survivor Guilt confronted me every lucid moment. I did not want to live. I was sad to the depths of my soul.

Barely conscious, I remember giving information to the doctors in the first few days. I mumbled my name, ID number, phone number, medication, and Charles' phone number. Friends and family would visit, and I would evaluate my memory by greeting them and saying their names. I would regain consciousness and find a childhood school, and Sunday school friend, Cheryl, whom I had not seen for decades, feeding me a spoonful of food. An ex-offender, written off by society, gently gave me sips of water and ignored the pipes and tubes in my nose and throat. The forever nurse inside me would talk to my head, "you've got to breathe deeper to avoid pneumonia. You've got to move position to avoid pressure sores".

Messages, flowers (one bouquet arrived from the man who had introduced me to the Lord Jesus Christ), and prayers poured in from far and wide, encouraging me to get well. I was aware of the distress of my daughter and grandchildren across the ocean in the USA, the unique needs of my two other adult-dependent children, and Charles, the rock-solid anchor in my life. However, something was stirring inside me. A conflict within. I had to fight my way back to life. Nevertheless, I was too exhausted to think or move, let alone fight.

> Disturb us, Lord, when
> We are too well pleased with ourselves,
> When our dreams have come true
> Because we have dreamed too little,
> When we arrived safely
> Because we sailed too close to the shore.
>
> Author unknown

Nestling in my Heavenly Father's lap

I was to learn that my God was present within my physical and emotional pain. One night while navigating my excruciating torture chamber (akin to some who endured the Spanish Inquisition), I saw myself crawling into my Father God's lap. I felt His arms around me. My God cradled me in His arms, and I slept. My healing had begun. Ever since that night, I often visualised myself crawling into His lap and resting. I had found peace within the tsunami's enveloping waves of the indescribable pain.

Charles – my rock-solid anchor

I was constantly exhausted those first few weeks. Charles was my constant hope. His presence never left me. He had to keep Rico and Lisa emotionally safe from fear and dread while coping with his feelings and the horror flashbacks. However, I could not keep my eyes open during the hours he spent watching over me. I exhausted myself trying to remember details – to this day, nothing comes.

Rico

My miracle son, Rico, had seen me three days before we left for the weekend camp. He was off work that weekend and is not one for camping discomfort. He needs his gadgets and electronics around him – a soft bed and a warm shower. So, he stayed home alone to look after our dog. He says he felt uneasy because we took longer than we said after he called me on the phone. When he called me again, there was no response. He was concerned because he had a driving lesson booked. Something was not right, he thought. A couple of my friends had turned up unexpectantly and then my sister Carol and brother-in-law Geoff arrived. They told him his dad would call him soon. Charles called and spoke to him on the phone, telling him there had been a horrific accident, Lisa was okay, and I was hurt and needed to stay in the hospital. He informed Rico that Charles would spend time at the hospital with me, but he should pack some things and go home with my sister. Lisa would join him there after they fetched her from the hospital. They would spend a few nights there. Charles informed Rico's workplace of the seriousness of the trauma, and he was given seven days' leave.

Rico's mind was in turmoil when he saw Lisa. She was covered in accident debris and glass. My siblings and their spouses had arrived, so Rico had them around him. He was shocked when he saw me in the hospital bed. I looked unrecognizable and was surrounded by all the emergency equipment. He said the "beep" of the life support machines disturbed him even more, and the seriousness of it all began to overwhelm him. My sister-in-law Beverley and a friend took him to the hospital chapel room to cry out his fear. During my months of recovery and frequent hospitalizations, he returned to his cheerful self. While I was learning to walk and limp in a shopping mall with him, he said he felt like my biological son because we were both walking so badly! This comment, not from the mouth of a "babe and suckling", kept reality to the fore. Rico still helps me put on my socks sometimes.

Vulnerability and learning – the tapestry's connectives

I learned that it is OK to admit my helplessness. To be completely exposed and vulnerable to others for all my basic needs. To depend on the care of others. To trust visiting strangers.

I learned that setting goals would get me on my feet again. I knew I needed to lean on others as mobilisation and physiotherapy started. It was OK to say, "please help me".

My leg and life were saved by an incredible orthopaedic surgeon, Dr Daan Botes, whom my God had placed in the emergency trauma unit that day. The next three trips to the theatre had the pins and screws inserted and skin grafted from my thigh to below my knee.

Steps – linking the tapestry's threads

First came the moving from a bed to a chair. How could that simple act be so scary but feel so good? I could not bear the weight on my legs. Fear of falling and breaking what had been fixed hindered me. We started with a walking frame (well before my dotage years!). One painfully slow step, two, then three. Day after day, mornings and evenings. I willed myself to do it. Still very slowly. However, I could not do any self-care activities on my own.

Robyn

My condition was still severe when my doctor wrote to Robyn's employer in the USA, asking that she be given special leave to come to South Africa to be with us. Miraculously, without Charles knowing, ministry partners worldwide responded and paid for her and my grandchildren's travel.

Nonetheless, the tsunami waves continued to advance. After eight weeks, our medical aid was exhausted, and I needed to be discharged to a step-down facility. However, Charles insisted that I come home. His employer kindly allowed him to work from home for the next three weeks while he cared for and assisted me with everything. I was still helpless - but not hopeless - Robyn would arrive in three weeks when Charles had to return to work. My God continued to weave the threads of my destined tapestry.

I had to be chauffeured 80km to Paarl and back twice weekly to change my dressings. One wound on the injured leg would not heal, and the doctor feared infection reaching the pin in my femur. It was resistant to every antibiotic. We switched to an unorthodox solution, and the dressings had to be changed every second day. Robyn is a registered nurse in the USA and took over changing the bandages. However, my leg refused to heal. Then my God dealt with the infection. Robyn was going to leave for the USA on Monday, and when she came to change the dressing for the last time, the wound was closed and dry. I was to see the doctor in two days. My God had again spoken peace in the face of my tsunami – the weaving of His tapestry continued.

Charles

Charles worked between home and the office for the next few weeks. We would time his absences for two hours to match my toileting needs. We had arranged for a physiotherapist to work with me at home, and I worked hard for the next sixteen weeks. Of course, there were times when the planned goal gave way to intrusive edges of the tsunami, but I was determined to become whole again.

I was helped up to the walking frame each time, practising one step at a time. Switching to elbow crutches was the next scary goal. Around and around the dining room table and furniture. Around the balcony. I was getting up and down from a chair. A neighbour would help Charles carry me down and up the stairs in a wheelchair to get to hospital visits and see a psychologist and a psychiatrist. I was carried up and down those stairs, seated in a wheelchair. Now that was a frightening journey. That is the way I went to my mother-in-law's funeral.

A hiatus before progress

I learned that it is OK to start all over again. A few weeks after being home, I could not tolerate food. Nausea and abdominal pain worsened, and I returned to the emergency unit, where my stomach contents poured out like ground coffee onto the floor. I knew I was in trouble. As a result of the soft tissue abdominal injury, a hematoma in my small bowel attached to my appendix and caused a total bowel obstruction. I was prepped for emergency surgery and told I would probably have to wear a stoma bag. I prepared myself for that. I could learn to live with that. I was desperately ill for the first few days. Then Charles told me someone wanted to visit me in the hospital and asked if he could bring her.

Luthando

I learned that dispensing grace and forgiveness frees you and the person you are forgiving. One of the tragic fatalities in my car was an eighteen-year-old man. Luthando was his mother's only son. Worse than my physical pain was the pain I felt I had caused this mother. But Charles gently coaxed me to agree he could bring her to see me. I recoiled at the thought of facing her. How was I to say, "I'm sorry!" But he would be there with me. I had never met Luthando's mom. Pamela walked up to my hospital bed with Charles. My heart lurched, and tears streamed down my face as she took my hand and bent over to kiss my cheek. "I'm so sorry," I repeated as we gently hugged each other. She told me to stop saying, "I'm sorry." She told me their best times were the last two months she spent with her son. She had lived through his teenage years in the troubled township in Khayelitsha, waiting for the police to knock at her door, saying that he had been killed in a gang fight or died from drug intake. Then his life changed when he met the Cape Town City Mission football team, and we started a mentoring relationship with her son. He was introduced to his God, the tsunami whisperer, and his life was dramatically turned around. God spoke peace into her son's life and her life and home. She thanked me that she knew he was in Heaven. I shook with grief as I was released from despair and guilt. She would see me again.

The tapestry takes form

Again, my God spoke to the tsunami. While I had recovered without a stoma bag, I lost my mobility gains and had to start all over again. But I knew it was possible this time. I returned to where I had ended.

Nonetheless, a few weeks later, one side of my abdomen started bulging. Tests revealed that my left oblique muscle had been completely torn from my pelvis, and I would need more surgery. I now host a large mesh patch in my abdominal wall, and I had to embark on another remobilisation programme. I had a support team cheering me on and bathing my feet, cleaning my mess, washing my hair, and picking me up off the floor when I fell. The star was Charles, who nursed me back to a relatively active life.

My next goal was to progress from two elbow crutches to one. Then one day, the physiotherapist announced that I was ready to tackle the stairs. Suddenly, that thought was much worse than the wheelchair trips up and down the stairs. I could not even take one step down without panic and shaking, but I began one step at a time. Every second day we would attempt an additional step toward goal seventeen.

During this time, I was healing in my mind as well. I was going to walk again. I knew it. On the night of Thursday, 31 December 2015, crutch in hand, the passage to my bedroom stretched in front of me. Like always, Charles hovered behind me to catch me before I hit the floor. "Stand close," I said, "I will not go into the new year on crutches. I'm going to walk into 2016 on my own." He took the crutch from me. I walked with small and stumbling steps but moved forward! My heart pounded, and I was exhilarated.

Charles and I went grocery shopping the next day (my first helpful trip), and I used the shopping trolley for support. I still do. Escalators and revolving doors at the malls petrified me. I was sure I would not make it on or off the escalator in time or that the revolving door would move faster than I could. But I had learned to say, "please help me" (remember?). I stopped at a revolving door one day, unable to take the next step. I asked a strange man to help me through. And it was OK! Then, we went on our first date night with friends. It felt so good to go out and have a meal.

I made the appointment with the psychiatrist to terminate any future follow-ups. I asked to be cleared to return to work. I had insisted that I did not want medication for depression. That I did not need psychiatric care. But I went several times to satisfy my doctor and the psychologist. She was unsure if I was ready to start my emotionally demanding work but agreed to let me try.

On 11 January 2016, I walked back into my workplace again. Three days short of four months since the accident. It was a miracle. The doctor who had saved my life was visibly moved when he saw me walking with difficulty but unaided for the follow-up.

However, the most significant benefit was the astonishment of meeting Luthando's mother. She was there to welcome me back and said, "don't stop. Many young men like my Luthando need you out there." Can you comprehend such grace? My eyes fill with tears just recalling that moment.

Chapter 9 is Lisa's story and a moving account of her lockdown experience. Readers will more fully understand how a tsunami impacted my youngest daughter and the emotional turmoil caused by mental illness. However, the presence and provision of my God provided a pathway from the forecourt of Dante's Inferno. The tapestry began to take shape but was still on the loom.

Chapter Nine

Lockdown casualty - Lisa's walk through the fire

The COVID-19 pandemic – a tsunami that still laps the streets of our cities - and the subsequent lockdown of the whole world caused additional mental anguish for countless people. Lisa's vortex of suffering during the lockdown tested and challenged my understanding of my God. I do not believe we will ever realise the extent of the mental health devastation caused by the pandemic and understandable gaps in reported and documented information.

Many people suffering with mental health challenges were lost in a frightening and mysterious cloud. Too much of the unknown unjustly imprisoned individuals in their scary world of unimaginable pain. We often heard about suicides, family murders, depression, and anxiety disorders. Social media was littered with fake news and misleading information about vaccines.

It is time that honesty challenged the destructive stigma surrounding mental illness. We must change the demeaning and hostile public narrative about psychological and psychiatric disorders. We must create a new mindset by removing the self-defeating protective mask – to pretend to be OK (to protect ourselves and our fear of embarrassment from how others perceive us). Mental illness is on the spectrum of humankind's maladies.

Lisa

I want to share one part of my precious daughter's depressive anxiety, anguish and tormenting nightmares. This is her story. Society-carved stigmata casts derogatory unjust shadows about mental illness. This tsunami needs an honest appraisal to understand how to walk through the fire with someone and come out with them on the other side.

You will recall me writing about Lisa's birth trauma that left her intellectually delayed, with mild cerebral palsy and on the autistic spectrum. She coped very well with life. She spent three months with her sister Robyn in the USA without us and had a wonderful time - but that was a long time ago.

The catastrophic accident happened when she was thirty-four years old, and I have already described that 2015 horror. Still, I have no memory of the tragedy. However, Lisa remained conscious throughout the frightening ordeal and she witnessed and heard everything. Can you imagine her raw terror? Furthermore, she could not run or move because she was trapped in a mangled wreck with death surrounding her.

Can we imagine Lisa's angst? She was a young woman trapped in a younger child's mind. She was petrified of hospitals and the sirens of police and emergency vehicles. Because of the carnage, the road was closed in both directions. Her worst fear became a reality when she was taken alone by ambulance to a place she feared - a hospital.

Charles drove behind the ambulances carrying us both; he was there when she was taken out of the ambulance and into the emergency unit. It was the worst day of her life and his. Yet miraculously, my God stepped into her tsunami and held back the wave from touching her body. Not a scratch. Not a broken bone.

She spent the next six weeks with my sister and brother-in-law in their home while I fought for my life in the hospital. She seemed to block out the horror. My sisters cared lovingly for her, supplied her needs and kept her active with things she enjoyed doing. Lisa loves colours and colouring pictures. Her colours on paper stayed bright, but the dark colours stayed trapped in her soul. She would not talk about her horror or visit me while I was in the hospital. We understood that and let it be. We had brief talks over the phone, and Charles would convey messages between us. Lisa would not talk about her trauma. Then, one day, she watched and listened to me count steps while I was learning to walk. She said, "Mom, I thought I was watching you die."

"In the accident?" I asked. She nodded. I held her, but she would say no more.

The new tsunami emerges

Lisa came close to bringing the trauma to the surface each time I had a new life-threatening emergency admission to the hospital over the next three years. During the full bowel obstruction episode, I was in agony at home and desperately ill. Charles was getting me ready to be carried down the stairs in a wheelchair to take me to the hospital. She was visibly distressed and started to cry, "Why don't you just die and get done with it?" she sobbed. We tried to hold and reassure her. But we knew where that cry came from. We could only entrust her to our God and the loving and understanding care of the wonderful elderly lady, Aunty Sarah, who helped care for us all. I could only begin to imagine the agony she was going through each time she thought she was watching me die. However, against the odds, I got better and came home each time, but Lisa's life of repressed emotions continued for five years.

COVID-19, Lisa and lockdown

The 2020 COVID-19 tsunami sent the world into an unprecedented frenzy five years after the accident. At midnight on 27 March 2020, South Africa went into total lockdown. It was freakish, and it terrorized Lisa. The sudden silence around us in our street, the absence of human contact except for our own household, face masks, visors, and sanitisers gave descriptive meaning to the adverse media reports. We had to turn the television off when the news came on so she would not see and hear the fear-mongering and negativity. The protective workshop for the disabled that she attended suddenly shut down. With other sufferers like her, Lisa's daily routine was turned on its head. Her mental health declined rapidly, pushing our family with her into a downhill spiral for the next two years. Where was my God? Where was Lisa's God? Charles often tried reassuring me, saying, "I see angels." But I was too profoundly broken to see angels right then.

At the same time, Charles and I realised that inactive retirement was not part of our brief. Three months after my retirement, I faced the lockdown realities confronting the desperate families in communities that we knew.

Many Non-Profit Organisations were forced to shut down. Acting on the insistent prompting of our friends Lorenzo Davids and Brad Sprague, we started a new Non-Profit Organisation called *On The Edge*. We knew we were crazy to listen to those two culprits at the time, but we did it anyway. We heard God's voice first, but we tried hard not to listen to Him.

Lockdown's impact

At the start of the lockdown, while Charles and I were on the road with our essential services permits tucked in our pockets, Lisa and Rico were in the safe hands of faithful friends at home for a few hours a day. Louisa and Colin made ministry possible by keeping things together at home. Lisa would want us to tell her exactly where we were going, what we would do, and what time we would be home. We had to be home before the designated hour to calm her anxiety. Charles would be at home if I was on the streets at night. Lisa and Rico would help me prepare food and hygiene packs for daily distribution. They were *On The Edge* volunteers in essential times and were occupied and safe from the fear and frenzy outside. Yes, my God was in the midst of the situation. However, Lisa remained in her deep well of unexpressed emotions.

Lisa refused to go outside but had always loved shopping for clothes and shoes! We coaxed her one day to buy a new T-shirt, but she first needed to get used to wearing her mask. After getting her into our car, I gently rubbed the mask against her cheek until she could tolerate it. Despite her trauma of seeing people all masked up, social distancing in queues, passing sanitising stations, and the spectre of face visors, Lisa chose her T-shirt, and we were out of there. But before we hit the accelerator pedal, we had to gently get Lisa into the car to go home.

By May 2020, the search for doctors began. On one of these trips to a doctor, Lisa opened the car door to jump out on a freeway. The child lock was always activated after that, but she would reach over to grab the steering wheel while we were driving. Every car trip was a nightmare journey. However, the next doctor's visit was due.

Lisa eventually became friends with her mask and sometimes joined us on a distribution run to help pass on packages and parcels. She tried so hard to understand what was happening around her. However, between May 2020 and December 2021, Lisa spiralled downward under the influence of a medical crisis and post-traumatic stress disorder.

Lisa, flashbacks and canine therapy

Five years after the accident, Lisa suffered from severe flashbacks. Lockdown had triggered the most profound anguish imaginable, and she refused to go near a car. Her days and nights were a living hell as she plummeted into suicidal depression. We were exhausted just trying to keep her from self-harm. Every sharp-edged item had to be hidden. She would be convinced she would not wake up when she fell into an exhausted and medicated sleep at night. "Am I going to die?" was a question she repeatedly whimpered. As her bodily functions began to slow down, she could not eat, and her weight dropped dramatically. Her depression was resistant to medication, treatment and psychological help. And my God was silent – or was He planning something else? Where was my trust?

In July, our neighbour gave us a puppy. A beautiful German Shepherd, and we saw flashes of Lisa returning as she held and stroked this canine therapist. We would help her throw balls for him to catch. We took him with us in the car so that she could sit and hold him while we drove to doctors' visits or when we could persuade her to have a lick of ice cream. Sometimes I saw only the tsunami and forgot about our tsunami whisperer, the Lord Jesus Christ. Charles would be the one to call me back to His presence. A mother's heart so quickly gives way to fear sometimes.

Plunging into the abyss, and my God raised His voice

However, as October ended, Lisa refused to go past our front door again. Fear gripped her every waking moment. She was convinced that the day would not end the way it started. That she would die. That some calamity would befall us all.

She had no sunlight on her skin. The sun stopped shining for her. We started a prayer group that would commit to praying for her through this fire. I posted updates regularly, with so much gratitude for these faithful friends. Oh, that my tsunami whisperer would begin to speak loudly.

Psychiatrists in the private sector had given up because of her depression's resistance to their medication attempts. In desperation, Charles and I took Lisa to the emergency unit one evening. I had a feeling that we may be missing something. I wanted to ensure that there were no underlying medical problems. My God had placed an insightful and conscientious doctor in the emergency room that night. He listened to our distress and grave concern for our adult-dependent daughter and he decided to run a blood check of her calcium levels. Her levels had rocketed. He told us that it was a medical emergency and was amazed at what had prompted us to bring her there that night. We knew it was our tsunami whisperer. While the September Spring brought new life outside, our precious daughter was battling a parathyroid crisis in the winter of her tsunami storm.

The CT scan of the thyroid area showed a large tumour on one of her parathyroid glands. Emergency surgery was needed, and she had to be hospitalised. She would not go home that night. Her terror was palpable. It was in the middle of level 5 lockdown, and as things were then, I would have to leave her in the hospital and not be allowed to visit. But our God heard our silent screams, and without asking, the hospital placed Lisa in a VIP private ward and said I could stay with her and that

Charles could visit to relieve me. That was a COVID-19-free space and they would not charge us for the use of that private VIP ward.

Lisa was in such a heightened state of agitation and anxiety that she did not respond to pre-anaesthetic medication. However, our Lord had prepared the way for us again. He placed one of His own - an esteemed surgeon who would operate on her. In the centre of intense lockdown protocols, he allowed me to dress up in theatre garb. I could accompany Lisa into the operating theatre and stay with her until the intravenous anaesthesia took the desired effect. I had asked where our God was – well, I am sure, dear reader, that you will agree that God was in our pain and trauma. Later that morning, after she recovered from the anaesthesia, we saw her smile for the first time in months. Lisa began to eat, and her stubborn cheekiness returned. She told the doctor that she wanted to go back home. "You will not keep me here, so that I have to pay for your nice car!" (Lisa has inherited some of her dad's chutzpah). However, that night, the terror returned. Her crying turned to heart-rending whimpering.

Then our Lord Jesus revisited her through this same surgeon, doing his nightly round. As he sat on her bed and held her hand, she said tearfully, "Doctor, the devil is messing with my mind." Then we saw something we did not expect in a busy private hospital, with staff stretched to their limits because of extreme COVID-19 challenges. This surgeon sat on her bed, stroked her head, and said, "Lisa, you are God's child. The devil cannot come near you. He is under your feet. Tell the devil that! When I entered your room, I saw an angel with a flaming sword guarding your room. You are safe. God is with you." Oh, my goodness, my jaw dropped as tears of gratitude rolled down my cheeks. Yes, my God was with us.

A change of tactics and then more changes

Finally, exhausted and having experienced a continuum of GO/STOP phases, we were referred to the state health service. We hoped that a multidisciplinary approach to her increasingly complicated challenges would help. That night Charles and I suffered as we had never before. We had no choice. We had to certify Lisa because of the increasing attempts at self-harm. It was the only way to contain her. We had to watch helplessly as they tried to sedate her without success. The medication doped her so much that she could not move, but she would not close her eyes and release herself to sleep. As she lay there, unable to move a limb, her mouth worded, "Am I going to die?" soundlessly, as her eyes followed our every move. Again, at the height of COVID-19 restrictions, the impossible was allowed. The doctors allowed us to stay with her until the sedative medication finally took effect. The emergency ward was overcrowded and chaotic; according to law, we had to leave her for seventy-two hours of observation. Charles and I left the hospital, and Lisa lay on a trolley bed in the middle of a ward with no screen around her. Emotional shrapnel and thoughts of the accident that I could not remember impacted her as I looked on. It was tearing my heart apart as we drove away from the hospital after midnight. But Charles had seen angels again, and my sobbing subsided.

Yes, our God was with Lisa. Early the following day, the emergency-duty psychiatrist called to say that after waking from sedation two hours after we had left, our daughter had paced the floor during the night. However, she responded to her questions later that morning. When asked how she felt, she said Lisa had summed it up, "Doctor, I'm tired of feeling so sad."

Then our God did the impossible again. The psychiatrist said that the in hospital COVID-19 conditions, the psychotic nature of many patients, and the degree of physical illness and injuries of others made it unsafe for Lisa to stay in the ward. Since I was a psychiatric nurse, they were prepared to send her home under my direct care and supervision if I felt I could keep her from self-harm.

However, they felt the best place for her referral was a hospital specialising in psychiatry with intellectually challenged adults. They would refer us there, but the waiting list was exceptionally long. They would adjust her medication, and I could monitor her and bring her back if there was any concern.

Then, my God did it again. He had prepared things long ago. The head of psychiatry called me after reading the referral letter. He had noticed the name Charles Kadalie as Lisa's father. He told me that as a young man, before becoming a doctor, he had visited the Kadalie home on many occasions when we played music, sang, and had band practice fifty years ago. He saw Lisa the following week. I remember telling him it felt like I was watching her drown but could not throw the rope for her to catch.

Lisa saw a psychologist but would not talk. She saw an Occupational Therapist and tried really hard. One day the occupational therapist told Lisa to choose a soft toy to take home to cuddle and hold on tight when going to bed at night. She should hold it and squeeze it whenever she was afraid. She chose a funny-looking multicoloured bear and named him

"Happy Boy". Happy Boy went into the hospital and everywhere else with her, and he is still an essential comfort when she goes to bed at night.

However, the medication was still not helping. The suicidal ideation and attempts and sense of hopelessness persisted. Catatonia was setting in, and Lisa could hardly eat but would ask, "will I die before supper?" She fell often and lost weight dramatically. She looked haunted.

Our old friends, Louisa and Colin, moved in to help us with her care and supervision. They were a real blessing at a critical time. Lisa trusted Louisa and was comfortable with her. She could be vulnerable with her. By this point, we were totally exhausted along with our daughter. As described before, our ministry in communities of need continued throughout the eight months of seeing our daughter suffer with no turnaround.

We feared Lisa would die as her bodily functions continued to slow down. Electro Convulsive Therapy (ECT) was our only option left now. I assisted with this in my psychiatric nurse training. It seemed barbaric fifty years ago, and I recoiled at the very thought of it. However, many patients get well. We had to try it. Dr Smith described how the procedure had changed over the years and was nothing like what I remembered. The hospital in the area we resided was heavily affected by COVID-19. The day Lisa was slated for admission, fifteen out of eighteen patients were COVID-19 positive and very ill. The doctors did not want to admit her because of the very real dangers and concerns.

ECT and from pillar to post and that amazing waffle

Our next hope was the only ECT facility at a private hospital in our area. However, we did not want private medical care because each profession was separate. Her situation was so complex, and we prayed for admission to the state facility - an academic hospital with some of the best multidisciplinary teams in the country. We prayed that the COVID-19 situation would resolve in time so she could receive treatment there rather than at the private hospital. But as we checked with the hospital weekly, the situation had not improved, and they could not take her.

In desperation, we got an appointment for the ECT at a private hospital. They were prepared to help Lisa as an outpatient. However, Charles and I did not have peace about it at all. Then God stepped into the situation in a very compelling way! The private hospital let us know that their ECT equipment had broken down. They could not see our daughter or say how long it would take to restore the service. That same week against all odds, the state hospital called to say they had prepared a "COVID-19-free" space, and Lisa could be admitted the next day! Coincidence? No! Our hearts soared with expectation and thankfulness to our Lord and Saviour.

I wandered slowly as a cloud … I saw

I remember taking a prayer walk in a forest opposite our home that afternoon. My God showed His presence through the trees. So often, God uses object lessons to speak His truth into my confusion and fear. The wind had been howling the night before, and one of the tallest trees had broken at the trunk.

I followed the upward-falling trail of the tall tree trunk because I wondered where it had crashed. The highest end of the broken tree had landed in the middle of a V-shaped branch. It was being held up by another tree and would not crash to
the ground. That was like our experience. Being held up by our faithful God and the love and support of those around us. Lisa, Charles and I would not crash to the ground. My God wanted me to know that.

Again, the most amazing doctors and staff were placed around us. Despite COVID-19 protocols, Charles and I could stay with her until she was sedated for the ECT and after she recovered. Nine times over the next three weeks, we watched her hand twitch. How different from fifty years ago. The first six sessions did not show dramatic improvement. Once more, Charles and I watched our shadows walk ahead of us back home without Lisa. They could not discharge her but wanted her to have three more ECT treatments over another week. Then, slowly, the change for the better began. We saw her take two steps forward and one step back as she returned to life.

The tsunami stood back, and a delicious waffle

She was discharged on 12 March 2021. Rico came home from work and gave her the warmest welcome hug. He, too, had suffered as he watched her suffering. We had to work hard to keep him safe emotionally and involve him in her care decisions. In true style, he came out intact. Discharged after three weeks in the hospital, our daughter slept peacefully with Happy Boy beside her for the first time during a tumultuous year of torment and suffering. She got to her bed, dropped down on her knees, thanked God and sent a voice note to Dr Smith to thank him. We joined her in grateful thanks.

For the next few months, we had to take things very slowly. Dr Peter Smith has followed her up as an outpatient ever since. God has just placed him in the right place for our daughter and us. We are forever grateful.

In January 2022, Lisa suddenly said, "I feel like a waffle." She got in the car and was unafraid and returned to the protective workshop a few weeks later and has been coping well. She still has a way to go, but we remain dependent on our God - He will keep her well. He has walked her through the fire and had his angels in medical dress stand before and behind her!

As we move into Chapter 10, the narrative weaves through the highs and lows of the inexplicable and unpredictable waves of persistent tsunami onslaughts. However, in parallel is the lesson that my God moves in mysterious ways, His wonders to perform.

Chapter Ten

Restoration

The highway accident resulted in Polytrauma. I had sustained severe injuries to multiple body parts and organ systems. The soft tissue damage to my chest and abdomen was severe. I was told I could expect complications to emerge up to three years later. Oh my, what will happen then?

No gain without friends, prayer and pain

I had gone for my last annual routine mammogram precisely a year before the accident. The following year was one of the multiple significant surgeries. By the end of February 2018, two years and five months after the accident, the next wave of the tsunami hit. However, my God was still threading His beautiful tapestry. I had many large lumps all over my body. Hematomas, calcifications, cysts, or necrotic fatty tissue were in abundance. The painful ones had to be drained, but I would learn to live with the rest. The ones in my breast were harrowing. So, with trepidation, I went for a mammogram. Something abnormal seemed different from the available evidence of damage seen, and a biopsy was scheduled.

On the day of the biopsy, Charles and I left for a ministry retreat with other leaders. The radiology specialist would call me with the biopsy results by mid-day the following day.

I woke up the following day in the retreat's beautiful surroundings but apprehensive. Later, as we were finishing a time of singing and worship, the worship leader began singing again just as we exited for lunch. I had one thing on my mind. I was expecting the call at lunchtime. But the words she started singing stopped me in my tracks. I had not heard the song before. It was Brian and Jenn Johnson's hit, "You're gonna be okay". My God had stepped up behind me and put His arms around me. I knew that feeling. I had crawled into His lap many times before. The words being sung spoke right to my fears.

However, I knew the expected call from the radiology specialist would confirm cancer – but I would be okay! The telephone caller broke the news that I had stage three invasive ductal carcinoma of the breast and that treatment needed to start urgently. Like a whirlwind, they set up appointments when I returned to Cape Town. Still, I thought of my late mother's brave but unsuccessful battle with cancer, and I had two adult-dependent children.

While Charles was his rock-solid self, I could not take much more. Then my God interrupted my drift towards melancholy with another superb timing intervention. Mergon Foundation, the fantastic organisation, had booked a Christian psychologist to meet with each couple. They had never had ministry leaders on a retreat with their spouses. This was the first time we had a psychologist meet with each couple, and Charles and I were first in the queue. Yet again, I had the opportunity to kiss the tsunami waves. Charles and I opened our hearts.

Next on the program was a walk and communion in the beautiful prayer garden. Ministry couples gathered around to pray with us for God's healing. One ministry friend, Neil, knelt at my feet, holding them as he prayed that God's healing would flow.

I was wearing open sandals with flower details, and he saw the flower open with life, not death. Three sequential events, perfectly timed, calmed our fears as the tsunami whisperer brought a sense of my God's presence and peace.

We were away on a retreat together for the next two nights without the children. We had time to process and think. I cried, and Charles prayed through what would need to happen next.

The following two weeks were a flurry of hospital appointments, tests and individual visits to specialist radiologists, oncologists, breast surgeons, and plastic surgeons. We pondered over medical aid quotes and treatment permissions. Friends and family worldwide began to pray, and fervent prayers came from within the prison walls where we had been working and from the broken spaces in our city. My friend Mariette told me someone had prophesied that I would be healed. My cousin Iris was also very anxious that I avoided chemotherapy and offered her life savings to try an alternative treatment.

I was scheduled to start the Red Devil chemotherapy in about three weeks. It would be nine months before harsh chemotherapy, surgery, and radium therapy would be completed. I prepared myself psychologically for the inevitable side effects and days of ill health. I tried to prepare my children, explaining the treatment and its side effects. I had some meltdowns and anxiety attacks when Charles and I were alone at night. I doubted that my body would survive this next onslaught.

The hospital where I was due to receive the chemo and radium treatment had "Vincent" in its name. I began to associate it with the ravages of chemotherapy. During the next three months, I prayed for ways to be a blessing and comfort to another woman who was more anxious than me. At the same time, the incredible movie about the life and work of Vincent Van Gogh called "Loving Vincent" hit our screens. My sisters and sisters-in-law, who were a great encouragement, joined me and urged me to shift from fear to the therapeutic stance of "Loving Vincent"! What a fantastic experience of art, song, and emotion! The theme song, Starry Starry Night, had never sounded more beautiful. I listen to it still.

I was booked to have the chemo port inserted in my neck for treatment to begin on 24 March 2018. The night before was agonizing for us all. But Charles and I had a standing Thursday night date with the group of former offenders we were discipling. We met every Thursday evening for a meal and an accountability discussion - our Accountability Table. These young men prayed with us.

So, it was the night before treatment was about to begin. We left this supper meeting and drove home after 2200. While en route, Charlie Bolton, our business mentor (Charles and I are network marketers with Neolife), called me and threw my carefully processed plans into turmoil. He said that while praying for me, God had told him to ask the doctors to give me eight weeks. To stall the chemotherapy plan, build my body up, and give it the means to fight this. I was totally thrown. I trusted this wise man completely. However, did he really hear this from God? What was his motive in sharing this? My life depended on it!

Charlie Bolton laid out precisely what he wanted me to do regarding my food and water and to max out on the super immune-boosting product that is part of our business. I was to take six times the average daily amount of what I knew was the world's purest, most concentrated, brightly coloured fruit and vegetable extract. I distilled my drinking water to take my usual supplements. We were talking about food and water all the way home.

By the time we got home, I was totally conflicted. I wanted this cancer gone. I had just come to terms with the chemotherapy due to start the following day. Now this call!

I could not move from the car. I had a total meltdown. I cried uncontrollable sobs while Charles just held me and gently prayed. We sat in the car inside our garage for nearly two and a half hours.

I started talking loudly to my God. A little too loudly, I must confess. I told Him in distress how confused I was. Did He really give Charlie, our business mentor, that message? I did not ask quietly but told Him I needed Him to show me from His Word what to do. I told Him I did not want to hear verses like, "By His stripes, we are healed" and "the prayers of the righteous will save the sick". I reasoned that I was conditioned to focus on these verses. I told my God to "give me a specific instruction from your Word!"

A thread from the Bible

Then it happened! Just before 0100 on 23 March 2018, we left the car and went upstairs. Charles was emotionally exhausted and went to our room. I sat down at my computer, still asking God for His instruction. I opened my laptop and just typed the word "healing". On my screen popped Exodus 23: 25-26. Not my regular go-to verse on healing. But "I will bless your food and your water, and I will take all illness from you … and give you a full life". WHAT? We had spent the last couple of hours talking about food and water!

Suddenly, a peace I cannot explain just coursed through me. I knew that God had spoken. I would not accept medical treatment for stage three invasive cancer. Excitedly, I called Charles to read this verse with me. The same thing happened. Inexplicable, total peace washed through his spirit. He said, "that's our answer."

We read the whole chapter. And I studied it in depth in subsequent days.

I was wide awake now, so at 0100, I typed an email that included the passage of Scripture to my daughter in the USA. I told her that my God had spoken. I would not start chemotherapy but follow God's treatment plan.

I then typed out the passage with highlighted verses for the medical team. The oncologist, the radiologist, the breast surgeon, and the plastic surgeon. I thanked them for their help thus far, but I told them God had spoken. And that in light of

His specific Word, I would refuse all further medical treatment. I would accept surgery if they continued to collaborate with me. But no chemotherapy and no radium treatments. They responded and warned me of the dire consequences because the cancer was in stage three and invasive and was HER2 and FISH positive. That meant there was a significant risk of it spreading. However, I assured them that God had spoken. I was at peace.

I had surgery in May 2018 to remove the tumour, which had shrunk and changed its shape entirely. They had no explanation for it. They said there was some mistake in the readings they had taken. But I knew better! However, there was a complication with the wound. It just would not close. It was a gaping hole. For the next four months, 24/7, I was attached to a vacuum dressing pump. I got used to telling people the strange sound, wrapped the tubes around my waist, hid it under my clothes and continued with my life and work. By August 2018, the wound was closed sufficiently, and I could discard the vacuum cleaner – another constructive dismissal issue!

A year later, I requested a CT scan for a no-cancerous spread. The doctor wanted to know if I would accept chemotherapy if the scan results did not give the news I wanted to hear. I said I would not. Well, then, "there's no point in doing a CT scan. Just go on with your life; you will just die of breast cancer," he said jokingly. We had reached that point of camaraderie! He told me to stop being a nurse and be a patient! So, there was no further discussion about the scan. But it would have been good to know.

I retired from Cape Town City Mission at the end of 2019. Robyn, my daughter in the USA, was delighted that I was finally retiring from ministry work. She surprised us with two tickets to spend seven weeks with her, our son-in-law and our five grandchildren. Oh my word, I thought this was life! For the first time in decades, I had no work responsibilities. I did not have to worry about statutory obligations, salaries, funding, and ministry programmes. It was pure bliss. I thought I could get used to this! We left for the USA at the end of January 2020.

Two weeks into our stay in the USA, we visited one of our mentors in Disciple Making, a five-hour drive from Robyn in Kentucky. We were to spend the weekend with Jerry Trousdale and his wife Gayle to discuss our story to be included in a book he was writing - The Kingdom Unleashed[65].

Oops

I woke early and doubled up with the severest abdominal pain. Nothing relieved it. We prayed, but the pain got worse. Our friends were older, and I did not want to disturb them, so we decided to wait until they woke up. Jerry took me to three walk-in clinics. They could not treat me because I did not have my passport. By now, Robyn, a professional nurse in Kentucky, had arranged for admission with a hospital in her hometown and told us to return quickly. A five-hour, excruciatingly painful drive later, I was in a hospital in Kentucky. The admissions doctor took my medical history and learned I had a cancer diagnosis and had refused chemotherapy. One of the tests he ordered was the CT scan they had refused to do in Cape Town.

---

[65] The Kingdom Unleashed. Jerry Trousdale & Glenn Sunshine. ISBN 978-1-73223999-0-6 DMM Library.

There was no sign of malignancy but lots of accident damage. Blood tests revealed severe pancreatitis with gallbladder involvement. The lipase levels in my blood were dangerously high, and they could not remove the gall bladder until they had dropped three days later. Morphine controlled the pain, and I was given intravenous fluids to lower the lipase levels. I had surgery three days later.

Amazingly, the surgeon asked Charles if he would like to sleep at the hospital. Of course, we loved that idea! We thought he would sleep in the chair, but to our amazement, they wheeled in a bed and placed it next to mine! How is that provision from my God whisperer of my tsunamis?!

I recovered well and went home to Robyn's. My granddaughter, Halle, started helping me exercise to increase my mobility. I noticed my ankles were swollen, so we upped the leg movements. By day two, I was like a balloon in congestive cardiac failure due to the fluid overload of all the intravenous fluids. I spent another few days in the hospital until I was cleared for discharge, with my heart fully recovered.

I spent ten days of my holiday in a hospital! My grandchildren made the experience fun.

The tsunami – a spent force

We had to leave for home in three weeks, and I was cleared for travel a week before. We had to be back in Cape Town on the 5 March 2020 because Charles had to officiate at the wedding of one of our discipled sons on 7 March. The world and South Africa went into the severest lockdown on 27 March 2020. We had made it home just in time. With the terrible trauma that my daughter Lisa had endured for two years, I cannot imagine our situation if God had not been in the timing of events.

Notwithstanding, on 6 September 2022, I had my fourth annual cancer screening. There was no sign of cancer. As I had said, my God had spoken.

Chapter 11 introduces an antidote to the ravages of the Apartheid tsunami and the destructive backwash from other tsunamis. I have pointed out the lacklustre performance of Churchianity and how many religious denominations have abandoned discipleship in favour of other motivational practices to get people to "come to church".

Churchianity is a heretical departure from the explicit goal of the church. The narrative will introduce the dynamic power of discipleship as a return to the mission of the Lord Jesus Christ for those who are his followers. We are not exhorted to "come or go to church" but to go and … disciple others.

Chapter Eleven

Kissing the political Tsunami and Jesus

At the turn of the century, Charles and I had invested many decades of our lives in the troubled Hanover Park community in pastoral care, youth work, community development and the many facets of aged care services. We had given it our all with no regrets. We had built life-changing relationships that impacted our home and family and coloured our worldview of contrasting dimensions - the rich and poor. We were part of a community that trembled under the socio-economic-political systems spawned by the destructive and inhibiting Apartheid tsunami.

The church met in homes, community halls and Cape Town City Mission facilities built in 1976. The GH Starck Centre for the elderly was opened in 1982. From then on, our church gatherings took place in the chapel of this Centre. The local community became part of the ethos and spirit of the home for the elderly. Many innovative world firsts broke ageing stereotypes and made active ageing fun. We saw transformations that crossed to the 3rd and 4th generations.

Our previous way of Christian ministry

Yes, we came to faith under the ministry of different people who would probably take time to understand this evolution of our discipleship ministry.

Yes, we, too, introduced people to faith in the Lord Jesus Christ. We worked and lived in a relationship with them and their families. We responded to needs and to issues of justice. We taught them the Word and to love God's word. We still have contact and relationships, and they instruct their children.

An evolutionary gap

However, we were frustrated by the shallowness of how the Gospel was lived out by many Church-going believers. There had to be more. We identified the gap between knowledge and active faith that inhibited individuals from sharing Christ with lost and broken people. The key to fruit-bearing was a close relationship with Jesus – not just reading books on "How to ...".

Before our change in approach, we, along with the conventional evangelical system, had stopped at Mathew 28.19. "baptize them in the Name of the Father, Son and Holy Spirit". However, we forgot to finish the chapter with verse 20, "and teach them to obey everything that I have commanded you" – discipling was missing. This was the method that Jesus established – discipling. We had it back to front. Jesus started a discipling relationship as soon as He met the disciples. He discipled them to the point where they acknowledged Him as the Christ. He allowed them to remain disciples despite their human frailties.

Charles and I deconstructed our church routine and way of thinking. We began to express our profound faith in our God differently. We laid down our traditional religion, church practice and head knowledge of the Bible and started understanding the reality of the Kingdom of God. We discovered the synthesis of loving Jesus and obeying His commands. Our God can draw men and women to himself when we get out of the way. In short, we made significant paradigm shifts in our religious thinking and how we lived out our faith. It was liberating, like restoring an oxygen line.

Harry from the USA

However, in 1995, Charles and I met Harry Brown, a mission leader from a ministry in the USA. We chatted about the Church and the impact of the Gospel amidst the brokenness in our world and community. Consequently, our kitchen table was to serve a new style of food for thought. We felt we were missing "something". Were Charles and I entering a mid-life crisis?

We pondered how the message of the Gospel had touched broken people and spaces with transforming power. Harry asked questions that made us think. "When will we be satisfied with our mediocre (no, it was not mediocre – just unsatisfying) ministry and churchiness? How were we presenting Jesus to a broken world? Had we deviated from the unambiguous instructions of the Lord Jesus Christ?"

For example, one day, Charles counted how many groups operated as a church or gathered in church buildings in the street where our church group met. He counted sixteen church groups in one street. Hanover Park was a highly churched community. Yes, many people were religious and needed God. Despite this active spiritual core, Hanover Park was Cape Town's drug and gangster capital. Children were desensitized to the violence they saw around them. What was missing? Where was evidence that "we are the salt of the earth and the light of the world?" Organisationally, we struggled with similar disconnects as our friends in the USA and other parts of the world.

A fresh voice from the church in Spain

My previous Cape Town City Mission Director, Lorenzo Davids, met with David Watson and a group of mission leaders in Cuba. They grappled with the same questions about presenting Jesus in a changing world. Consequently, in 2004, Lorenzo asked Charles to stand in for him and attend an international meeting with mission leaders in Spain the next day! Miraculously, Charles managed to sort out his administrative issues and obtained a visa in one day. Charles has the gift of the gab[66] and charmed the staff at the Spanish Embassy with song and soccer speak, and his visa arrived!

For the next week, he engaged and prayed with a small team of God's servants worldwide. After the first night's gathering, he called me excitedly and said, "I know what it is that we've been missing!" At the end of the four days, he called me, saying that the message entrusted to the Church would never be shared the same way again. Our ministry and lives have never been the same since.

David from the USA

David Watson spent time with us in Cape Town to guide our direct engagement with God's Word. We learned from his God

---

66 He has never been to the Republic of Ireland to kiss the Blarney Stone.

story. We began deconstructing our method of sharing the unchanging mission of the Gospel[67].

By His words, "Peace, be still," we began to push back the life and soul-destroying impact of the Apartheid tsunami crippling the spiritual lives of people branded as society's outcasts. We began to learn about the heart of Jesus.

We discovered how much we, too, had complicated the pristine Gospel with our subjective taboos. As members of the global Church, we, like others, had added unnecessary baggage to its mission. The words of Jesus in Matthew 23 enlightened my evolving understanding of my God.

The Jesus approach

As Charles and I pondered Matthew 23, we discovered gems of wisdom that enabled us to understand that the message of Jesus to his followers contrasted with the practices of the Pharisees[68]. They had failed to practice what they preached. We also read how their misunderstanding of religious teaching had led to making religious observance a burdensome ritual and a selfish preoccupation that resulted in a "holier than you" disassociation from helping those in need. Of specific note, too, was the presence of hubris in the lives of the religious leaders of the period. Oh my, when I ponder how I had emphasised traditional interpretations at the expense of what the Gospel was about, I am amazed at the patience of the Lord in enlightening me.

---

[67] Val and Charles outlines this journey when referring to Matthew 18.
[68] See the seven woes in Mathew 23.

This reality struck home when I thought of those who now espoused the so-called prosperity cult, where everything is about prosperity, the love of money, and being bigger and better. Sadly, much of 21st-Century Christianity is about tradition and subjective interpretations of the Gospel.

Furthermore, modernized Christianity places more value on knowledge of the Bible but not enough on obeying its commands and living by God's instructions – a theoretical understanding compensated for a practical commitment to Jesus. The emphasis is on issues not in any way seeded by the Gospel.

The message of Christ is often preached with no regard to the full-orbed paradigms of justice, mercy and integrity. So, in concert with those who had already started on this necessary focus on discipleship, Charles and I embraced spiritually enriching changes.

We realised that our ministry must not force people to commit cultural suicide to be Christ-followers. The Great Commission is for ALL, wherever and whoever they are, right where they are. Broken communities and people who are at different levels of seeking and turning towards God need living evidence of the transforming power of the Gospel. Most people whom we disciple do not have a church-cultured background. So, we are careful not to extract them from their families and communities and rush them to a church. The natural risk is that they will too quickly adopt a culture of churchianity that will make them very different from the host culture of their family or affinity group. Instead, we prefer to build them into small communities of faith where they are coached, mentored and discipled into spiritual maturity where they discover who

God is and His design for their life. Sometimes that may be a church in a building. But often, it is not. Our focus is on intentional disciple-making that moves at the speed of relationships.

This process we know globally as the DBS or Discovery Bible Study (or discussion) is our primary tool. It builds spiritual DNA in a new follower of Jesus to ensure:

- Their life and development are crucially rooted in the authority of God's Word and the Holy Spirit.
- That prayer is a lifestyle, not just a weekly prayer meeting.
- The responsibility of caring in ministry to others is for everyone, not just the pastor or a select few.
- That if we say we love God, we have to obey Him.
- Sharing what we learn from God is as natural as breathing.
- We must live in an accountability relationship with others to help us obey God's instructions.
- We can bring an awareness of God into our everyday conversations without being offensively religious.

So discipleship is about walking with people on their journey towards Jesus without removing Jesus' influence where it is needed most and is often the most difficult; their own home and community or affinity group.

We learned to enter a broken community as servants, not professional, scalp-hunting Christians. We learned how to earn the right to heal brokenness, address lostness, recognise the

Person of Peace, and stay in a relationship that models Jesus. This concept of appropriate evangelism made so much sense. We moved from evangelising everyone who will listen, even those not ready to hear, to a Jesus-style approach. We learned to pour our lives into the few who will listen, be willing to take a spiritual conversation further, learn, obey, and share what they know and then live in an accountable relationship with others.

Lessons from a clock

In one of the most valuable learning experiences at our seminar, we were tasked to assemble a plastic clock with about sixty-eight disparate pieces of plastic shapes made in China and suitable for children aged six years and over. We, seasoned ministry leaders, had to build this clock in small groups and get it ticking as a team within 30 minutes. We had no instruction manual to start with. That came later. Talk about church splits! Well, as we debriefed, we came to understand that anomaly.

So, no matter how gifted, talented, or academically trained we are, we do not own God's work. We must know the heart of the designer and follow His instruction manual. When receiving a new cell phone or electronic device, we often tear off the wrapping, open the box and discard the first thing we see, the instruction manual. We use the most prominent features: stop, forward, rewind, and play, but we don't know the power in the designer's mind.

Of course, like many others, Charles and I were enthusiastic about introducing the genuine Jesus to hurting and broken people. However, we had to retrieve the instruction manual again - the Bible. Our cities comprise people whose needs are becoming more complex and diverse. So, we found that building a clock was not easy. We would have to ask for help from others.

Consequently, just as we threw all the parts of the clock on the table and tried to figure out how to get it ticking, we would have to deconstruct the way we do church and be the church!

Subsequently, we realized that all the parts, even the most minor, seemingly insignificant, make the clock tick. So, in ministry, every single person has a role to play. Not just the pastor, church leader, deacons, elders, and so on. We had to entrust Kingdom work to others – to delegate. We had to learn to take chances with people. To develop their leadership skills and inborn natural gifting to serve a place in God's work of redemption.

However, if a part is missing from the clock, it will not work. We must search for the missing piece. But you cannot search for it if you do not know it is missing or refuse to acknowledge it. In our ministry lives, we must search for the missing parts.

Stealthily, David swapped the tiniest clock parts between groups as we all argued about who was right or wrong, whose strategy worked best, and who was and was not doing their part. Meanwhile, frustration levels rose as the time deadline ticked closer. We had to get this clock ticking.

We learned that extra parts are useless to the clock but may help others build their clocks. One person/group/organization /denomination does not have everything needed for the transforming movements of the Gospel to happen. We must find the ones with the right parts to make the clock function. We must learn to cooperate with others, get the needed components, and make the clock function. Transformation in our city would require each of us - but not without God. We must find where He is working and join Him in His work. Our world and cities are in trouble – a sense of urgency is needed.

Then, David, without warning, swapped the groups around. Our work was left hanging! We looked on with shock as the next group undid all our complex and sincere work. They thought they knew better and began building the clock again. Time was running out. We realized that If something in our representation of the Church is not working, we must be prepared to undo everything and start all over. That sometimes someone else will have to finish what we started. That someone would find a better way that worked. And we learned to be comfortable with that. There is no place for hubris in ministry – pride hinders progress and obstructs the work of each member of the body of Christ – the church.

We began understanding Jesus' precise instructions in Luke 9 and 10 and Mathew 10. We were getting ready for another dimension in our faith adventure. We understood the life-on-life transfer of living in obedience to the teachings and instructions of Jesus. We became increasingly involved in discipling people in a non-religious but Jesus-like way. Over the next few years, we were helped to understand this more fully. We spent time training, observing, and practising with the giants of faith; we saw lives transformed by the unmatched power of the touch of Jesus on a broken life.

Learning to unlearn

Alvin Toffler[69] put it succinctly in Future Shock. He wrote, "the illiterate of the 21st century will not be those who cannot read and write, but those who cannot learn, unlearn and relearn. It will be those who do this best who will be the ones to inherit the future".

That got me thinking about our present reality and the accuracy of the Aristotle Complex[70] when we react from "a complex ... of unconscious behaviours, emotions and feelings that condition the way of behaving and thinking[71]". An example might be how we discipline our children. We replicate the pattern of control of our parents/carers to keep order (c.f. how I punished Robyn when she was "cheeky" and how my mom had reacted when I gave her lip).

Carl Jung's formalisation of Aristotle's idea[72] was evident in the challenging adjustments to the COVID-19 Pandemic. We changed from "this is the way I do things" to "this is how I must now do things". Indeed, a complex and costly transition for most of us.

Path dependencies

There is no doubt that we often, unthinkingly, follow precepts and practices that were passed on to us. We all inherit and learn from cultural influences. We gain knowledge and experience from our primary caregivers, teachers, and childhood

---

69 Future Shock by Allan Toffler (2022) Ballantyne. ISBN: 978-0-593-15947-7.
70 See Aristotle Complex by Clark, A (2021). https://psychoques.com/aristotle-complex/#:~:text=The%20Aristotle%20Complex%20is%20a%20psychological%20condition%20described,be%20verified%20or%20are%20adjusted%20to%20the%20circumstances.
71 c.f. Clark, A (2021)
72 Aristotle and Jung at https://www.reddit.com/r/Jung/comments/butt6c/aristotle_and_jung/

relationships. In my situation, I gained experience when I received the new flag of Apartheid South Africa.

Similarly, we clothe ourselves with the images of the church. We unthinkingly fail to think critically and distinguish between the traditions of history and the reality of the church's mission as detailed by the Lord Jesus Christ.

Path dependencies are shaped by 'lock-in' effects which shoehorn communities into positive or negative pathways of change. "Structural lock-in effects", "economic lock-in effects", and "socio-psychological lock-ins" are significant. These factors make specific community pathways impossible to implement and can be severe hindrances to raising community resilience[73].

Charles and I, for example, had to unlearn the ramifications of our learned church concept, our business operations and how we handle domestic complexities. The new learning required we actively understand the pros and cons involved in the change process. We had to acknowledge that we had not followed the teaching of Matthew 18 – we now needed to take responsibility for our actions and move forward.

Charles and I include the following principles to keep us on level ground.

1. Prayer is a lifestyle, not a routine.

---

[73] Wilson, G. A (2013). *Community resilience: path dependency, lock-in effects and transitional ruptures.*
https://www.tandfonline.com/doi/abs/10.1080/09640568.2012.741519?journalCode=cjep20#:~
:text=Path%20dependencies%20are%20shaped%20by%20%E2%80%98lock-
in%E2%80%99%20effects%20which,communities%20into%20positive%20or%20negative%2
0pathways%20of%20change.

2. Our God's Word is dependable.

3. The Holy Spirit is our guide into all truth.

4. Love God and love all people. Even those who are complicated to love.

5. Prioritise family and keep our children as part of our journey.

6. Take chances with people and encourage them to minister to others by, for example, sharing Bible readings and taking responsibility for their lives. To do this, we seek to model aspects of discipleship.

7. Let God take the lead and trust in God even when the way seems unclear and chaotic.

8. Seek where God is already preparing a group, a community, or a person of peace, with signs of a readiness to hear and take spiritual conversations further. Then get into step alongside God. Let Him take the lead. He owns the vision. He said, in John 15:5 paraphrased, "I am the vine, you are the branches. If you abide in me and I in you, you will bear much fruit". Thus the onus is on the believer to focus on her/his crucial relationship with the Saviour.

9. Abide in Christ with faith and hope regardless of the situation.

10. Lay aside titles and discard barriers that stop people from experiencing God's grace and love.

11. Love justice.

12. Treasure integrity.

13.   Laughter is medicine. God relieves the heavy moments with His incredible sense of humour.

Chapter 12 removes the theoretical gloves of discipleship. We will discover illustrative facts about the often-missing dimension of discipleship. Some might view this process as a prelude to "soul winning". We begin by walking alongside those who are like sheep without a shepherd[74].

---

[74] John 10.

Chapter Twelve

Putting Discipleship Together and Empathy

David Broodryk, a global disciple-making coach from South Africa, points out that we cannot hope to address a person's lostness until we have addressed their brokenness.

Charles and I have always maintained that we have no right to challenge any person's spiritual condition until we have acknowledged their brokenness, pain and daily struggle.

Effective discipleship requires time, respect, and listening to someone's story with compassion and humility. We must step out of our comfort zone and identify with the disharmony of the other person's life and daily struggles.

For instance, Jesus debated within the clinically austere precincts of the temple and sat with the "top brass". He also walked alongside the ostracised lepers, scared and hurt humanity, and took his disciples with him. By listening and communicating alongside others, we can shine Christ's redeeming love of the Saviour who was tempted in all points like we are[75]. The Lord Jesus Christ's approach contrasts

---

75 Hebrews 4. 14-15.

markedly with the Pharisees' examples and many modern concepts of "soul winning", where adding another scalped trophy to the witnessing wampum belt marks the route to the soul-winners award – and a boost to an ego fed by numbers.

However, Frederick Lowe had arrived with the Gospel message amid the mayhem, chaos and injustice of political madness, and he went about doing good. When he died, the City Hall was packed with mourners. Now, as one of the world's most complex, socially contrasted and divided cities, the discipleship of the early disciples during the harsh Roman times needs to rise up and march throughout South Africa. Every Christian (the called-out ones) is part of the church. It is time that the church went to the people. The stories in this chapter reflect pain, deep hurt, shame and degradation. We must address the root issues if we ever want to see a healed and transformed city and country ... "go and make disciples, teaching them to ...[76]."

We must be able to find the person of peace in every segment and affinity group in our complex city, as Jesus instructed His disciples to do[77]. When you see this worthy person, stick with them, transfer your life into them, and equip them to transform from their broken spaces and bring hope and healing in those spaces to Jesus. Work with the few so that they can reach the many - disciple-making principle - that began some 2000 years ago in what is called Israel today.

We were asked by a major denomination in another province to spend time with their teams on the streets. After that, we were to debrief with their leaders about how they could best

---

[76] Matthew 18
[77] Luke Chapters 9 and 10

engage the brokenness around their church. They had to choose between building a wall around their church or changing their strategy to practically engage the brokenness around them. The team I took with me were like those mentioned in Chapter 12. Having been restored from their brokenness, they gracefully guided theologians to look at their city through the eyes of Jesus. They were the inside leaders of broken spaces.

One night, we were on the streets having conversations of hope with young women prostituting themselves in the area around this church. It was freezing cold. As I talked to one young woman, I saw her shivering in her skimpy, short dress. At her invitation, I started to pray by holding her hands. Then, as I bowed my head, I saw her almost bare feet covered by a thin shoe on the cold pavement. "Do your feet feel cold?" I asked.

"My feet are very cold," she answered.

I replied, "If I give you my warm socks would you put them on your feet?"

"I will appreciate that very much," she responded. Then it dawned on me that the damage from my accident prevented me from taking off my socks when I had nothing solid to hold onto. So I called Charles over and told him what I wanted to do.

He bent down, took off my thick warm socks and asked her, "Would you allow me to put these socks on your feet?"

"Thank you," she said.

Charles knelt down, took her feet in his hands, prayed our God's protection over her, and then gently fitted my socks on her feet. Her eyes glistened with tears at a man's first gentle, nondemanding touch in a long time. I know what a compassionate and caring touch can achieve in making it possible that broken chords will vibrate once more.

Discipling – the highways and byways

To illustrate this next part of my tale, David, whom I spoke of before, quoted an African proverb from the novel Things Fall Apart (Chinua Achebe[78]), "until the lion learns to write/tell his story, the hunter will always be glorified".

May I share the stories of our heroes? These pioneers from our discipleship ministry will bring joy to our lives until we breathe no more. Theirs is the story of the Kingdom of God driving out darkness. The transformative power of the Gospel that Charles and I longed to see when we first started deconstructing our concept of "church" is dynamic. They are the lions; one day, they will share their stories in print. These stalwarts are among those whom I wish to honour. They taught me so much about the practicalities of discipleship. Not book theory but discipleship on the ground.

Sibusiso

The wedding we officiated at (we rushed back from the USA) was a celebration of Sibusiso's story. Thankfully, for the one hundred guests present, the COVID-19 lockdown occurred just after the occasion. His best men were ex-offenders too. He was a man who was Cape Town's most wanted criminal in 2001, but through the discipling process that I have described, he became a trophy of God's grace. He has taken many others who were just like him and introduced them to his Saviour, Jesus, who

---

78 Chinua Achebe (1958).

had spoken peace and calm to his stormy and broken life and made him whole. He was the inside leader, the person of peace about whom we had learned. One day he asked me, full of emotion, what we wanted from him in return for our love and time investment in him. In the underworld, his life, something had to be given in return. I looked into his eyes and said, "give us more, Sibus." Eleven years later, he is doing just that. I saw him climb a mountain in another province to find his mother, who had abandoned him when he was eighteen months old. He took us later to meet her. I saw him forgive and release her.

Mvuyisi

I saw Sibusiso enter a drug den and lead Mvuyisi, a drug lord, to faith and hope in Christ. Mvuyisi was an outcast and hated in his community, as they blamed him for the crime and robberies perpetrated by young people addicted to drugs. The community inhabitants decided to take justice into their own hands and brutalized him in a mob justice attack that left him with an eye gouged out and nearly dead.

However, Sibu started conversations of hope with him. In his drug house, he got the drug lord's fingerprints on the Bible. He taught him to have simple conversations with God and discuss life and God, not religion. Customers would come to buy their drugs. Mvuyisi would put the Bible down, serve his customers, and pick the Bible up again.

I saw this drug lord come to faith in Christ too. I saw Mvuyisi lead his girlfriend to faith in Christ. The first time this dealer and his girlfriend started praying together, they would stop and laugh uncontrollably at each other in the middle of their prayers. They could not believe what they were doing. Charles conducted the wedding of Mvuyisi and Alime in our home with amazed family and neighbours witnessing this transformation.

It was miraculous. Today Mvuyisi is a role model, and mothers in that same community ask him to help their children. His wife has just graduated with a BA degree in Psycology. Their little son is named Charles!

Mbuzeli and Cecil

One of our expectations is that, as we take someone by the hand on this faith journey, we want to see whose hand they are holding. Mbuzeli was a friend from the underworld who was still in prison. He criminally ruled a large, troubled community. He used to supply the weapons for Sibu's past criminal activities. Mbuzeli was still in prison when he saw Sibu's Facebook pictures. His friend and co-accused looked completely different from what he remembered – he was engaged in positive activities. "What's going on?" Mbuzeli asked from prison. He could not believe or understand what he was seeing on Facebook.

"When you come out, look me up, and I'll tell you," Sibu answered him. Mbuzeli contacted Sibu on his release, and Mbuzeli heard his incredible transformation story. That is when Charles and I were introduced to this next hero Mbuzeli. He was older than the other parolees. Mbuzeli learned to trust us and shared his dream of becoming a boilermaker. He had done some courses in prison, but because he had a criminal record and was still on parole, finding a college that would enrol him took a long time.

However, we eventually found one, and he completed his boiler-making diploma. During this time, he became a follower of Jesus too. Then he needed to have an 18-month internship certificate to affirm his qualification. But we hit another brick wall. Eventually, with his brother's help in another province, he secured an interview with one of the newer power stations. He called me from there because the application asked about a criminal record. "Tell the truth," I said, "we must trust God with this." They called him for a second interview to hear about this criminal record. He called me again and said, "Val, what an opportunity I had to tell my story." He has just signed his second five-year contract. During the COVID lockdown, he flew down and brought me a monetary gift to help others who followed behind him. That is the Jesus transformation about which we speak.

Mbuzeli then took Cecil by the hand. He was another young man who had been active in criminal activities and had been arrested with Mbuzeli. So it was that Mbuzeli led him on a faith journey too. Together, they have launched and run a Christian Non-Profit Organization in the same community they used to terrorize. Feeding and caring for the poor and those marginalized in their society. They were captured by love and grace and now freely share God's redemptive message with others. They were not extracted from their community when they began their walk with Jesus. Their friends, family and community saw the transformative power of the Gospel in action. They saw change happen before their eyes.

> And seeing the man who was healed standing there with them (Peter and John), they could say nothing against it[79].

---

[79] Acts 4:14

In 2017, our team of formerly incarcerated young men were asked to take over the soccer academy in one of Cape Town's prisons. That was a new playing field for us. We facilitated the soccer lineups and games with the direct help of a wonderful prison warden. However, we also taught about life using soccer as a tool. We prepared the young, incarcerated men to value life. We introduced them to the concept of God, who valued them and had a purpose for their lives. We helped them understand that they did not need a go-between but could connect with God directly through a relationship with Jesus. We invited them to contact us on their release. Sadly, some returned to prison, and others were killed. Yes, prison and gang life have a tight hold from which only God can deliver people - discipling is emotionally draining.

Athenkosi and Cameron

Two more remarkable stories came out of this soccer room. They were in the cells together. Athenkosi was already a seasoned prison gang member and initiated Cameron, the newcomer, into the prison gang. Cameron was released about two years earlier than his gang member friend and cellmate. Upon his release, he was taken by the hand of the heroes I mentioned before. Cameron experienced faith in Christ and a remarkable life change.

Meanwhile, Athenkosi, his former prison cellmate and seasoned prison gang member, had come to faith in Christ through the prison-held Discovery Bible discussions in the football room. We were privileged to witness the miracle of change in our swimming pool two years later. On his release, Athenkosi was baptized by his former cellmate, Cameron, whom he had initiated into the prison gang. We had lots of laughs around the baptism pool that day.

Cameron

Cameron had a problematic and impoverished childhood. He had no close relationship with either of his parents, and his father became a vagrant. Cameron had dropped out of school very early in life and got involved with street life. Later, guns and criminal activities landed him in prison for five years. He joined the soccer team, where his life began to change. One of his dreams was to return to school after his release. But he was twenty-three years old. We could not find a school to take him to the basic starting level he needed. We finally found an adult learning centre that would start at the very beginning to teach him to read and write.

This 23-year-old had the guts to return to school and start at level 1. Cameron can now confidently read, write and speak English, Afrikaans and Xhosa. The reticent young man we worked with in prison has blossomed and confidently speaks to large and small groups. He has two years before he writes his matric (Grade 12) certificate. Then he has a dream of entering a Hotel School. He has always dreamed of becoming a chef. One day I was preparing a meal for him while he sat at my kitchen table. He said, "Mama, one day you will be sitting down, and I will prepare an amazing meal for you." He works as a casual at a fast-food chain to support himself and is a wonderful, compassionate young man.

Cameron searched for and found his homeless father, whom he forgave. This young man cared for his dad until he died in 2022. His dream, besides being a chef, is to play the violin. He bought a secondhand violin and is putting cash aside for lessons. Charles teases him and calls his music dream "from violence to violin." Cameron is now also the Department of Education spokesperson, promoting the school and sharing his life story. Everyone deserves a second chance. Jesus instructs us – the seventy times seven kind of chance.

Athenkosi

Another young man was raised without his parents' love and care and lived in an abusive environment. Athenkosi was shifted between family members in different provinces. He started criminal activities at a young age and received thirty-five years in prison when he was seventeen. Some sentences ran concurrently, and he was released in his 29th year.

He was a violent and angry young man at the centre of vicious fights with other prisoners and prison officials. Many scars today tell those stories. On 6 January 2021, he was released with ten years of parole. Charles and I continued our journey with him on the outside. We have watched him grow through his anger. He is now a follower of Christ and a role model to young boys in his community with whom he has started a soccer team. He is now speaking life into them using a soccer ball to introduce conversations about God. We enrolled him on entrepreneurial training, and in July this year, he launched his little location restaurant from a container. So, where a dumping ground and a waste area for fights and robberies once was, he now proudly manages his kitchen. He worked with Charles learning some skills and work ethics, and used that money to build his "restaurant". At the launch of his business, the head of the prison where he had been incarcerated spoke to guests about this "troubled, angry and often uncontrollable young man whose life change was dramatic". However, like the others, this lion needs to tell his story, and I hope it will be published when appropriate.

Some questions

How will we stop the cycle of recidivism if we cannot change our attitudes and practices as representatives of the church, business, and learning institutions? There is a seed of good that can be cultivated. But we have found that these doors of opportunity are shut in their faces. Yet my God is the seventy times seven chance giver. So many good programmes run within our prison system, but the challenges evoke concern.

We must increase the level and variety of support along developmental lines when young men and women are released from prison. Failing that, all the good that may happen on the inside falls flat on its face on the outside.

Fatherlessness dramatically contributes to the vast majority of these broken young lives. We need fathers, mothers, and mentors who open their homes and hearts to broken men and women. It is a huge task and not without risks. However, to see and experience even just one of these many stories makes the life-on-life discipleship investment worthwhile.

Rebooting to find the connection

It has become natural for many in the church and Christian ministry to define success by the numbers and visible results we can see. We seldom measure ourselves against what "ought to be" in the light of Jesus' instruction to disciple others.

Matthew 28:16-20 instructs us to go where He tells us, not to where it's easy or comfortable for us; to trust and worship even when we are doubtful and afraid; to go in His authority and to know that He has given us that same authority; to make disciples of ALL people - no one is excluded from His grace; to make them followers of Jesus.

We do that by allowing them to live alongside us and transferring our lives by following Him in every circumstance; baptizing them is an instruction given to His disciples that means us, ordinary followers of Jesus, not just the select few. It is not a specially timed ceremony. Baptism, in the name of the triune God, is a natural step of obedience and evidence of the new birth into the body of Christ. We see friends baptising their friends and family members baptising each other. Then CRITICALLY teaching people to OBEY the commands of Jesus. That process changes thinking, value systems, actions, and relationships with others and is transformational across generations.

Many have taken the five-fold ministry FUNCTIONS (cf. Ephesians 4) and made them TITLES, creating a bottleneck for disciple-making. We think planting a church means putting up a building. Still, the minute you put up a building, you immediately slow down the replication of disciples. Efforts get ploughed into maintaining the building and managing the structure and programmes. Discipleship demands that we shake the dust from our feet if they do not accept our peace – we cannot do that if we are stuck with a building.

Any experience of serving in God's kingdom is unique. Obedience to His Word and His instructions are fundamental. The wisest disciple-maker I have learned from used to tell us that Churchianity is for church people. Disciple-making is for lost people. There is a vast difference in the way we introduce them to Jesus.

Chapter 13 is for Rico, our precious adopted son, who remains a cornerstone of humour and transparency. Furthermore, Rico is a product of discipleship. Charles has suggested that I warn readers to expect the unexpected – the evidence of reality in one young man's life.

Chapter Thirteen

Discipleship and learning from laughter

I would like to share some of the many occasions when laughter stood face-to-face with tsunami waves. Some incidents are, however, unprintable!

As parents, we had to be like circus acrobats to keep ourselves and our children together. Travelling was one of these balancing tricks. We often kept them out of school to further their world education. More than once, we came back from our travels penniless but so much richer.

Now Rico, our son, is a social animal and has caused us so much laughter. Charles is like that too. They make heavy days light for people.

The elevator pitch[80] - Keep It Short and Simple (KISS)

The communication experts will teach us about the Elevator Pitch. The concept challenges a salesperson to present their product to fellow elevator users during the time it takes the elevator to take her/him to the destination level. Now Charles and Rico have perfected this art – whether requested to pitch

---

80 See: https://corporatefinanceinstitute.com/resources/career/elevator-pitch/

or not. Charles will step into an elevator, face everyone and pipe up with, "Isn't this a beautiful day God has blessed us with?" As individualistic as ever, Rico will announce, "Hello, everyone, this is my mom. Her name is Val."

Who knows where discipleship can begin?

> Gracious words are a honeycomb, sweet to the soul and healing to the bones[81].

Rico's escapade – "I am the winner"

The preschool he attended had a sports day. His very first. With his marked leg discrepancy, he could not hope to come anywhere near winning this race. On your marks, get set, and GO! And he was off! We cheered him on wildly, but the rest of the field was already at the finish line. He ran his heart out, oblivious that the race was over. Seeing no competition as he approached the finish line, he pumped his fists in the air screaming, "I'm a winner, I'm a winner!" Many years later, we cheered him on wildly again to watch him win swimming GOLD at the SA Games for the disabled.

Queen's guard

I love London. I studied and lived on the corner of Oxford Street and Berner's Street at a hostel linked to the hospital. It was like living in the centre of the world. One year we took the kids on holiday back to the old haunts. If you remember his story, Rico has a marked leg and foot discrepancy. While he loved the buzz of the city and the London Underground, he was already physically tired from hobbling around London. However, I wanted to show him the spectacle of changing the guard and

---

81 Proverbs 16.24

Buckingham Palace. A Queen's Guard was stationed directly across the street from us. Still and motionless. Rico was convinced it was a statue. No amount of explanation would convince him otherwise. Suddenly, he hobbled at full speed across the road to "touch" the statue and prove us, liars!

The Queen's Guard was caught off guard. How could he have anticipated this crazy child's actions?! As Rico reached within touching distance, the guard lowered his gun menacingly in front of him, barking out, "STOP AT THE ARCHES." A shocked and petrified Rico shouted back at the statue - the Queen's Guard! "Dammit, you scared the s..t out of me!" He hobbled at full speed back, for me to wipe his tears while we convulsed with laughter.

Amtrak

We were on Amtrak, travelling across the USA from West to East. Rico had a blast making friends with anyone who would show any interest. He is wired that way and quickly charmed the onboard train attendant. It was a safe enough time and place to let him wander and chat with people, so we kept an eye from a distance to ensure he was not a nuisance to anyone. Then he was gone. We knew he had to be somewhere because he could not have left the train. I was about to panic when we heard his voice greeting everyone and welcoming everyone on board the train over the train driver's intercom. He had asked the train attendant to meet the train driver!

Meet the pilot

We were flying between states in the US. Again, Rico was charming the air hostess. It was before the world went crazy and pilots were locked in. He summoned the air hostess at cruising altitude and asked her if she could take him to meet the pilot. She promised to see what she could do. A little while later, she came to fetch him to meet the pilot. Soon after, we hit some turbulence, and the plane gave a distinct bump. Charles got up and apologised to everyone, "That's what happens when you give my son the controls!" People start talking to each other when they lighten up.

Chocolate pudding

Racial sensitivities still plagued our land when Charles and I took our kids on a much-anticipated holiday weekend. The hotel sits in what was still a traditionally White part of the Western Cape. We strolled through the tourist shops below and entered a shop with many fascinating craft items on person-high shelves. Lisa and I were browsing while Charles kept Rico amused. Or so I thought. Then I heard Rico greet the white lady at the checkout counter. "Hello, pudding!" She greeted him and thought he was the cutest thing she had seen in a long time. They were having a roaring conversation in no time. The black lady assistant heard the conversation. Curious, she poked her head around the side of the high shelving to see who her partner was talking to. Seeing the black face peeking at him around the corner, Rico greeted her, too, "Hello, chocolate pudding!" I saw Charles disappear from the shop, leaving me to deal with any fallout. Fortunately, they both howled with laughter, and I did not have to apologise too much! He was a welcome visitor for the rest of our stay.

A bus trip to Harlem

We were in New York City, but I wanted to experience Harlem's vibe with its working culture, restaurants, and its music. But I wanted to take a bus in peak traffic with workers making their way home. So that is what we did. The bus was packed with commuters heading home, but we could not sit together. Charles and Lisa sat a few rows ahead of Rico and me. The bus was a hotpot of people chattering across the aisles, much like black township IsiXhosa conversation style back in Cape Town.

I was looking at the street scenes through the bus windows. Rico was listening intently to the conversations on the bus. Suddenly there was a lull in the conversation, and the bus quietened. His voice rang out, "Mommy, why did Jesus make them black if they speak English?" Why did Charles always pretend not to know us when Rico spoke out the unfiltered thoughts in his head?

You can laugh now

Rico has had many major orthopaedic surgeries to correct the congenital deformities from his ankles to his hip. After one, he was placed in a body cast from the lower chest to his feet. Can you imagine confining him to a body cast for six weeks? Well, a therapist suggested a skateboard. He positioned himself face down on one, and then he was in paradise, narrowly missing the staircase many times! A later surgery to stop the growth in his healthy leg had him on crutches with his one leg in a plaster cast. I decided to take him to the movies. We entered the darkened cinema and walked down the steps to our seats. The next thing I knew, his crutches flew, and he tumbled down the stairs. I was mortified. Had he damaged the recent orthopaedic procedure? The cinema was completely silent while I helped him regain his crutches. Next thing, he faced the audience, gave a wave and said, "OK, you can laugh now!" So that is what they did.

A Disney strip show

One of the live shows in an amphitheatre at Disney world was pumping, and the crowd enjoyed the music. Then they mistakenly asked for volunteers from the audience to show off their dancing moves. Of course, Rico's six-year-old hand shot up, and he was called to the stage. Without hesitation, he was up on that stage, ready for the music to start pumping, and he danced to the crowd's applause. Then, because he was getting hot, we saw him take off his hoodie, twirl it around his head, and throw it into the crowd – followed by his T-shirt. By now, the audience had warmed to him and cheered him on. Thankfully, the music ended before his pants flew into the crowd! He did not learn that from me!

Manager's award

When Rico was a little boy and had started walking unaided, we battled to find shoes that would work for him because one foot was three sizes smaller than the other. However, one gentleman with a senior position at a large retail clothing store heard about our struggle. He had a pair of shoes specially made for him by this retail store. Oh, my goodness. It was the most beautiful pair of boy-child shoes I had ever seen. Navy blue and red. One shoe sized six and the other sized three - a perfect fit with some room for growth – and Rico was excited beyond himself.

As he got older, we could get around this challenge if the ankles of the shoe were high enough. He always wanted to work at this same retail chain. After he finished school, against all odds, he

 successfully interviewed for a job in this retail chain store. Apart from marked dyslexia, he has no social filters while being a social animal. We did not think he would last two weeks in a work environment. But it has been nearly ten years. One day, he called me from work to say he had received the Manager's Award. He came home with a tongue-in-cheek look on his face. The award read, "To Elrico Kadalie – Manager's Choice Award for always saying the wrong things at the wrong times". His certificate still has pride of place in his room, and he still has his job.

That middle muscle and applying for a driver's licence

I have what Rico calls my "evil eye." It is the warning look that I give him when I anticipate something inappropriate is about to slip out of his unfiltered mouth. He had to apply for a learner driver's licence. Still, he had to do the test orally because of his reading and writing limitations. Our processes require a doctor's certificate to validate why an oral examination is needed.

He had complained about tenderness and swelling over the breast region for some time. He would not accept my explanation about the hormonal activity. He thought he had cancer. I thought it best to pay the doctor once and get two things done simultaneously.

Doctors behind closed doors, preparing for a driving test and the allure of legs

Now, this doctor had a runner's dream legs. She walked into the waiting room to pick up his folder, wearing summer wedge heels that defined her perfectly sculpted calves. In my next life, I want a figure like hers! "Mommy, who is THAT?!" he leaned over to whisper in my ear.

Forgetting that he had never personally met the locum doctor, I asked, "What do you mean. Have you never seen her? She is the stand-in doctor".

"Do you mean SHE is going to examine me?" he whispered. My evil eye locked with his as I warned him to behave himself.

We were seated at the desk across from the doctor as she introduced herself to him, "I know your parents very well, but I haven't met you. How can I help you?"

He responded, "Oh, there's nothing wrong with ME."

I leaned over and whispered in his ear, "we HAVE to tell her." (I was referring to the fact that he battles to read and write because of the foetal alcohol damage and so needs her certificate to get an oral learner driver's licence.)

"No," he growled back at me.

Squeezing the words out the side of my mouth into his ear, I repeated, "We HAVE to tell her why we're here." Then, facing the doctor, I said, "Doctor, he needs to do an oral learners test, and we need a certificate from you to prove it's necessary."

She had not dealt with him since he first came to be part of our family. So she had no idea of his medical history. All she saw in front of her was this sociable, confident 21-year-old boy full of testosterone.

"Why do you need to do the test orally?" she asked, puzzled. I knew Rico had no intention of telling her.

He left me no choice, "He has severe foetal alcohol challenges that affect his reading and writing proficiency," I said.

Rico leaned forward, planted his arms on the doctor's desk, looked her full in the eye and seriously said, "Doctor, she knows all the damage she's caused, and she still won't stop drinking!"

I doubled over with laughter, and the doctor was perplexed. She had no idea that I had problems with alcohol! I saw the look on her face and, between the laughter, told her that I was not his biological mother and not the cause of the foetal alcohol challenges.

Rico changed the subject. "I DO have pain and swelling in my chest."

I told the doctor that he did not believe me when I told him it was hormonal, "But since we are here, would you check it out?"

Here comes trouble, I thought as she directed him towards the examination couch. I growled in his ear, "Just behave yourself. I can hear every word."

I heard her explain to him while palpating his chest that it was hormonal swelling across one breast area. When I peeped in, I could see him squirm.

Examination over, he plonked himself next to me. While the doctor was washing her hands and preparing to sit across from us at her desk, he whispered in my ear, "Mommy, I really had to speak to my middle muscle on that couch!"

I cracked up. The poor doctor must have thought I was crazy; others might still think I am. In my defence, I refer such enquiries to the writer of 1 Corinthians 4.10.

Narrowboat adventures

Since childhood, I have loved Cliff Richard, The Shadows, and The Beatles. Cliff and The Shadows would perform together again in 2009 at Wembley Stadium, fifty years after they first performed together. I had to be there! I persuaded Charles that I would forego birthday presents for the rest of my life if he would take me to see them live at Wembley Stadium. We made a holiday of it. We hired a narrow boat for a week and cruised down and back up the Thames for seven glorious days. Just the two of us on a 60-foot, 20-ton steel narrowboat.

We were given a thirty-minute lesson on throwing anchoring ropes to moor the boat. We received instructions on manoeuvring through the locks and between the multi-million-pound yachts. We had breakfast sailing past castles and talking to swans. The beauty spoke peace to our souls as we appreciated Aunty Doreen, who was at home with Lisa and Rico. I suppose you must love and enjoy each other's company to be trapped on a narrowboat together for seven days and nights.

At the end of the seven idyllic days, we went to experience Cliff Richard and The Shadows at Wembley Stadium, full of grey-haired rock n' rollers! I conveniently did not tell Charles that

Cliff and The Shadows would perform in my hometown at the Kirstenbosch Gardens in a few months. I have not had a birthday present from Charles since. But the narrowboat experience for both of us made it so worthwhile.

The next chapter will address the importance both Charles and I have in our mindsets about the disruption caused by transition points in our lives. I emphasise the importance of moving towards convergence when things come together and purpose becomes known. We are challenged to let go of toxic life experiences and abide in Christ so we reproduce good fruit that lasts.

Chapter Fourteen

Mindset[82], transition and focus

We have had many transition points in our lives. No doubt you have had those too. Some, like retirement, are planned. But nonetheless, daunting because, for so many, their identity is wrapped up in their job or title. We have learned from all our tsunamis to keep our core identity in Christ alone. Our stint as voluntary patients in a psychiatric hospital helped us realize so powerfully that apart from our identity in Christ, everything else is expendable. We could let it go. Other transition times crash over you without warning. Nothing can prepare you for it. Transitions are seldom comfortable. For us, they have been downright unsettling most times.

Down but not out

Once, a large and powerful freak wave hit me off my feet. As my feet left the ocean floor, I was spun in every direction. I had no idea whether I was facing up or down. Or moving left or right, and I was disorientated. But a friend saw me drowning and, grabbing my legs, pushed me up to gasp for air and find my balance again. My feet were on solid ground once more. So too,

---

82 Philippians 2. 1-11.

it has been in unsettling transition times. Friends, family, and faith partners have grabbed hold of us and helped us reorient again. But above them all, when dashed by tsunami surges, our unmovable Rock was our Lord Jesus Christ.

A diamond and a windscreen

Learning to let negative experiences with people go was often the hardest thing to do. We have experienced our highest joys in ministry; those times were easy. But we have also experienced the lowest of times. We have lived through hard times, character assassination, unfair accusations and bewildering betrayal. I often had to answer my "why me?" with "why not me?". Those are the dangerous times when I risked allowing anger, indignation, and hurt to worm into my spirit and psyche. I had to learn to let go of what did not belong in my mind and soul and know who God is and who I am in Him.

I had a potent reminder about this and the wonders of the human body. Four years after the accident, I noticed a hard pimple on my upper arm for the longest time. At first, I thought it was a simple blackhead. But it would not budge, so I ignored it. After a year, it suddenly felt sore and started inflaming. It felt like a boil. Strange, I thought. I went out and bought some ointment to draw it out and covered the now painful and enlarged pimple with a "boil plaster" for the recommended three days. It was sore by the second plaster change but seemed as if it would open. So, I pressed around the edges to get the "abscess" out. But instead, out popped a piece of my windscreen! Five years after the accident! It looked like a diamond! I shouted excitedly for Charles to see what I had on the gauze – the bloodied edges of a diamond-shaped windscreen piece. Charles retorted that the missing hubcap might soon come out of another part of my body. As I reached for the plate to crack over his head, we burst out laughing and saved a dish from the skip – this was one Thelmarism act I have not repeated.

But God gave me an object lesson then. About the process of making a diamond. Dirt. Pressure. Heat. Charles and I had tasted all of that through the catastrophic times in our lives. God was just shaping and forming us like a diamond.  As I looked at that piece of the windscreen, I reflected on the fact that our bodies, made in His image, instinctively know what does not belong. No matter how long an unacceptable foreign mass is inside us, our bodies will eventually force it out. If our minds and emotions were like that, we would not live in a world with so much pain. Charles and I try hard to get those we work with to get out of a victim mentality and to stop blaming apartheid for the decisions and choices they make.

I plan to make a necklace with that windscreen piece - a constant reminder not to hold onto things I should abandon. Evidence that the omniscient, omnipresent and omnipotent God of tsunamis sees me in whatever state I am in and wherever I find myself. Like Hagar cried out in her distress, "Jehovah Roi - God who sees me."

We moved house on the 20 June 2022. After twenty-six years of memories, transformation stories and conversations around my kitchen table, this was a significant transition. My "God who sees me" pointed me to some of my most incredible learning experiences in that house.

> Because of the L*ORD*'s great love, we are not consumed,
> For his compassions never fail. They are new every morning;
> Great is your faithfulness.
> I say to myself, "The L*ORD* is my portion;
> Therefore I will wait for him[83]."

Seedless grapes and discipleship

Nature has taught me lessons about transitions too. I would watch our grapevine in its different seasons and remain intrigued by how it switched to accommodate the starkly different seasons.

Can we picture a vine as it drapes across the supports in the vineyard? Can we envisage the vine's gaunt ugliness as a naked and tangled mish-mass of twigs in winter? Seemingly lifeless. Have we watched the pruning process and wondered if it will grow again? Stripped down to nothing.

Ah, but spring growth arrives, and the first buds will appear, and we can watch the green leaves grow and spread visibly day by day. The barren twigs disappear amidst a mass of the flourishing green bouquet of green trumpeting the magic of a promised summer. As summer approaches, the bunches of grapes will cling like rhesus monkeys to the perfect and mature branches ready for picking. We juice these grapes each year,

---

83 Lamentations 3. 22-24.

and from the pulp, my nephew Russel, an avid gardener, has more vines sprout from the seeds.

This parable is about discipleship. We can only reproduce who we are. Of course, genetic modification now produces grapes without seeds that taste and look the same as grapes. However, only grapes with seeds can reproduce. So, if we abide in the divine vine,[84] we will produce grapes – with seeds. Each season has its place and purpose. And every winter gives way to spring again. So it has been in our lives, and that is discipleship – to reproduce.

Lesson from a fruit farmer

We had a magnificent old avocado pear tree in our backyard. Year after year, we could feast on the best quality avocados and homemade guacamole, with more than enough to share. For two seasons, the avocado pear tree did not bear edible fruit. We tried everything to feed the soil around it but had little result. The other fruit trees seemed to be struggling. Charles and I took a weekend out in Elgin, a fruit-growing region. We decided to look up a local fruit farmer for advice on what we could do to feed the soil with the perfect nutrient concoction to see our fruit flourish again. Then my God taught me another lesson. The farmer told us not to strive to make the growing conditions perfect. The tree must struggle to grow strong and bear good fruit through harsh conditions. Whoa! John 15 hit home, and I pondered what it means to abide in Him and He in us.

---

[84] John 15. 1-11.

Anchored

I once watched a colossal oak tree during a typical Cape Town south-easterly wind. The branches near the tree top bent and swayed wildly in the wind, but the trunk did not move. I was reminded that abiding in Him and His Word was key when my faith faced the tsunamis of life. Indeed, without Him, I can do nothing. So, as we allowed our fruit trees to struggle a bit, we learned not to take people's struggles away from them but to assist them in growing through their struggles - discipleship.

The end of another lap around the block

I finally retired from full-time ministry with the Cape Town City Mission at the end of December 2019. My dear friend Mariette has headed up the Board of City Mission during my time at the helm. In 106 years since Frederick George Lowe started the City Mission, it was the first time that two women led this legacy-filled mission organization. Mariette as board chair and I as the reluctant chief executive officer. This was a time of massive organisation restructuring. I had to hold it together and turn the focus back to disciple-making.

Two worlds merge in Christ

Mariette, the director of the Cape Town City Mission, and I are from culturally and professionally different backgrounds. I was a professional nurse and she was a psychiatric social worker, and a colonel in the Apartheid tsunami's Defence Force.

Mariette had moved to Cape Town from Pretoria (the seat of Apartheid ideology). During those early days, she shed many tears at my kitchen table as we sensitised her to the dark reality of Apartheid. Charles and I became her first Coloured house friends, as she jokingly calls it. Our relationship has grown into a friendship. Her heart beats for the work and ministry of the Cape Town City Mission and for us in our new post-retirement ministry role.

Another lap around the block begins

My God had other plans as I reflected on the "what does the next season look like for me?" Walking the long transformational road alongside broken and hurting people and raising them up as leaders had become a lifestyle. You cannot retire from that, can you? So, sixteen weeks later, with a little push from our friends, we launched a new ministry called *On The Edge* at the height of the catastrophic effects of the national lockdown.

Our *On The Edge* enterprise exists to take people on a transformational journey of discovery with the Lord Jesus Christ. We do this in collaboration with other disciple-making movement leaders. We share with hurting people on the fringes of our city, equipping them to become leaders of change in their own areas of influence to bring about generational change and transformation.

Understandably, social, political or religious movements typically involve many people mobilising for the same goal or outcome. Things go "viral" quickly; if one leader is removed, another will take the vacant post. We cannot always be rigid about planning our day. So, we anticipate disruption, constantly evaluate, and, if necessary, begin again (cf. Chapter 11 - the clock). Arguably, Christian discipleship is driven by a passion for a cause. Charles and I function well in this kind of space.

My seventy-plus year and tsunamis

The tsunami waves have somewhat abated, and my journey has become less complicated and calmer. I have seen the stories converge to a point where my God's purpose and calling are clear. However, I will continue to trace the hand of my God's faithfulness weaving through the swells and ebbs of future tsunamis. When the subsequent tsunami hits, as it surely will, I will draw strength from knowing how He has held us in every other time of trouble. I will trace His faithful hand in every story.

As I see His tapestry, I know that the Lord Jesus Christ is the eternal rock against whom I have been flung by the tsunamis seeking to destroy my life and family. My God has not moved – the Lord is indeed my shepherd …

The next Chapter introduces my Facebook snapshots of the complexities of our fractured city and exposes avaricious and prevailing injustices. Still, we must deal sensitively with the legacy of Apartheid and understand what it has done to our nation's psyche.

The content will show how the path-dependency of the Apartheid creators still impacts our society. To change the metaphor, the Apartheid tsunami, like COVID-19, has left South Africa with the strains of long COVID. We remain a divided country. Nonetheless, crises always come with opportunities to serve and to walk into broken spaces with Jesus Christ, the disciple-maker, as He restores, heals and transforms those who call out to Him.

Chapter Fifteen

Lockdown, Personal Reflections and Discipleship

I finally joined Facebook in January 2008. I enjoy the memories that pop up. So, it was sobering going back to my earliest posts. I was intrigued to read my emotional responses and personal observations to things that disturbed me and made me angry or happy. Apart from personal crises, there was a distinct shift in my mood when COVID-19 and the worldwide lockdown began. Most times, my social media posts were angry rantings projected against the few who controlled the world and the injustice I saw and experienced every day.

I will share a written collage of edited snippets from my Facebook thoughts (and other observations) that reflect on a segment of society that Christian discipleship must address. Well-intentioned tracts, megaphone sermons, and the "how to do" approach do not reflect practical discipleship. Religious leaflets are not always culture-sensitive – and, therefore, meaningless to some readers. Loudspeaker blasts rarely result in discipleship. Broken people require an empathic understanding before mass proselytizing takes place. We must remove the barriers (the leaflets and microphones) separating us from those for whom the Saviour died. We must engage in the privileged, walking alongside discipline with those without a shepherd.

Anomalies and ethics

While children died of hunger and wars raged on, honest businesses closed, and families lost their livelihood and ... and ... and.

> The wealth of the world's top ten richest men has more than doubled to $1.5 trillion since the pandemic started[85].

The COVID-19 industry was reported to be around £10,000,000 per year. Who are the beneficiaries? What were the non-economic costs to individuals in developed and developing nations? Why did 1+1 not make 2 anymore? Why? Why?

The bitter taste of injustice blasted my senses during that period. Maybe it brought back memories and feelings of times in my past. In 2014 Charles and I were driving on the West Coast Road R27 when we were struck by the jagged edges of the prevailing corruption, injustice and politically motivated priorities in our city. We watched cyclists, joggers, and people walking their dogs for the longest stretch of specially built, tarred, street-lit cycling and jogging roads. In contrast, we had just been in Khayelitsha, where raw sewage ran down the streets in many areas. We heard about a school falling apart in Nyanga that would only be repaired in five years. The Apartheid tsunami, deactivated under President Nelson "Madiba" Mandela, still ghosts South Africa.

---

85 OXFAM in NEWS 24.

> "O that justice and righteousness would flow down our streets like a river.[86]"

The lockdown restrictions were scary enough for adults. Still, for our adult-dependent children, it was catastrophic as death stalked homes and streets. All this talk of death and funerals introduced gloom and insecurity. Our house had always been full of people dropping by for tea. Suddenly the walls echoed with silence, and we could not visit anyone.

However, my God gave me something to laugh hysterically about that first lockdown night! I had enough extra food to feed about fifteen people. I asked Charles to take the meals to a spot in Parow where many homeless folks spend time together. I wanted to go with him, but he said not under the current circumstances. So I packed the food, some disposable plates and forks. He went off with strict instructions about social distancing and keeping his disinfectant close by.

He pulled up at the accustomed space, and a young woman emerged from the makeshift shelter. Charles rolled down the car window, greeted and asked (in the expressive Afrikaans language), "Hoeveel is julle[87]?".

She immediately responded, "Vi jou Pa, honnert Rand[88]."

For a few seconds, Charles was clueless, then he realised what she meant and promptly said, "Nee man, hoeveel mense is julle hier. Ek het warm kos gebring![89]."

---

86 Amos 5.
87 "How much (many) are you".
88 "For you pops one hundred rand"
89 "No man, I mean how many people are here! I brought some warm food!".

She apologised profusely, but Charles (the brave man with the pickaxe handle) was so taken aback that he sped off without praying with the woman after delivering the food. He returned to normal when he arrived home laughing and told us the story. Rico and I howled with laughter.

Disturbing days

In the townships, impossibly long queues snaked everywhere you looked. People pay a terrible price for being poor. Social grant recipients stood for hours without seating, refreshments, or water being provided before receiving their allowance. There were no chairs for the old and disabled. The long queues needing social grants, groceries, and transport were heart-breaking evidence of the disparity between the "have's and the have-nots", and we were powerless to do anything.

I saw a day hospital queue stretching some 200 people in length. Very well controlled with social distancing, but not a seat or refreshment option in sight. No wonder our news reported two older persons dying in the queue.

It was just past midnight. I reflected on a whirlwind week. Although we lived under the flight path to Cape Town International Airport, it was eerily silent. Where were the planes?

Social distancing? What's that? How is it even possible when ten to fifteen people cram into a shack? Strangely COVID-19 did not decimate these populations of the poor. I was convinced that their living conditions made their immune systems more robust.

Disturbing days or opportunities for discipleship

With Essential Services Permits, Charles and I could access the streets for relief work at any hour.

I pondered the stories of the pragmatic Jesus who, according to the Bible, made it possible for the multitudes to have food[90]. Christ empathised with his audience – a core component of discipleship.

The Cross amid zero-hours contracts

On day 10 of the lockdown, I received a call that poor communities on our beautiful West Coast struggled to feed their families. Many were cleaners, farm labourers and domestic workers and were unpaid during the lockdown. We met grandmothers who were raising six to ten children. Where are the parents, you ask? Well, that is another discussion.

By the end of that day, distributions and all that went with them were done. We headed home one and a half hours away. The N1, a national road, was spookily deserted - as was the area where we lived. Two days prior, we saw traffic officers with speed cameras trapping on both sides of a nearly empty N1! My jaw dropped in amazement.

Humankind was brought to its knees by the sinister virus, COVID-19. Still, as we pulled into our street, the brilliance of the illuminated CROSS erected on the Tygerberg Hills greeted us. Ah, I pondered, this is why discipleship is needed – to carry the message of the Cross of the Lord Jesus Christ into the highways and byways of every city, town, village and hamlet. As I gazed

---

[90] Matthew 14. 13-21; Matthew 15. 32 – 39; Mark 6. 30-44; Mark 8:1-13; Luke 9. 10-17; John 6. 1-15.

at this iconic reminder of hope and salvation from my window, I felt the impact of reassurance touch me – my God's angels were around and about.

Trapped – the other side of the coin[91]

With other ministry partners, we contacted young women caught up in prostitution. These dear people, trapped in a demand-supply cycle of risk and need, were from South Africa, Zimbabwe, Namibia, and Nigeria. Lockdown had a debilitating effect on them too. How would they pay their rent, eat and ensure their immune system was spiced with fresh fruit and vegetables? How would they send money home to support their family? Social distancing was necessary, but …

My heart was drawn to six young women spaced along Voortrekker Road. We returned home to pick up some hygiene supplies and returned to find them - but others had taken their place.

"How are you coping on the streets during a lockdown? How do you keep yourselves safe? Where do you stay? Where are you from? What brought you to the streets? Do you understand what's going on right now? Do you understand the precautions you need to take? Do you know what to look for in yourself and your clients?"

"I really want another life. I don't want to be here. But right now, I'm stuck here."

They answered us respectfully, describing their plight and gratefully received the hygiene packs. This was not the most

---

[91] 'There's no protection': South Africa faces Covid legacy of sex for money (msn.com)

appropriate time to have said to them, "Jesus loves you," and handed them a tract to read and then leave. The relevance and the language of "good works[92]" is a non-judgemental message demonstrating love, time, and compassion – discipleship.

> If a brother or sister is naked and lacks daily food, and one of you says to them, "Depart in peace, be warmed and filled," and yet you give them nothing that the body needs, what does it profit? So faith by itself, if it has no works, is dead. But a man may say, "You have faith, and I have works." Show me your faith without your works, and I will show you my faith by my works. You believe that there is one God; you do well. The demons also believe and tremble.[93]

However …

One night on a popular radio station, they were discussing the role of social media in spurring the incitement behind the recent unrest and anarchy happening across our country. The person being interviewed was a respected journalist.

He made a statement on the radio that made me splutter with indignation. He gave what he said was a legal definition of incitement and then gave an example, "If a prostitute (stands on a corner) and raises her skirt, that constitutes incitement!". Good grief, did he incite me as I reached for a plate to crack on his head!

The pathetic patriarchal comment of the journalist reflects the ridiculous mindset of many males. Even worse, the lady presenter interviewing him let that go unchallenged! Thus,

---

92 James 2. 15-19

testosterone-filled, macho men will defend themselves when lust fills their loins, and they cannot keep their trousers on or zip closed. Their window shopping turns to pay for the product.

So, where does this immature but destructive male mindset come from? Let us look at the Creation story, Adam, and Eve[93].

Adam was given a job to be the gardener of the first paradise. He needed a helper to meet the job description requirements, so the Creator took him aside, extracted one of his ribs, and made Eve.

The divinely sculpted couple had responsibilities, and one was not to eat the fruit from one specific tree.

Eve and the serpent were chatting (oh, the danger of careless talk, strangers, and believing fake news!). It is no wonder James 3 is about "the tongue", which rarely features in sermons.

Nonetheless, the wily serpent used Eve as the supply chain to carry the forbidden fruit to Adam. I keep reminding Charles that the fruit was not identified as an apple and has nothing to do with using the technology of that name!

Remember that the responsibility to work in the garden was core to their employment. So, Adam took the fruit and WOW – it was delicious!

That evening when the couple was supposed to report back to the Creator, their Creator had to find them. He did and asked Adam why he had not kept the diarised appointment.

Adam replied that he was naked and afraid to check in for the meeting.

---

[93] Genesis 2:4-3:24

Responding to the further questioning of the Creator, Adam (the first man) blamed Eve. He did not admit he had been irresponsible – and said, "the woman you put here with me gave me some fruit from the tree, and I ate it."

Oh my, he was caught out. Adam resorted to a double defence to rationalise the situation and defends his irresponsibility. He blames the Creator and Eve. Sadly, many individuals still play the blaming game and fail to shoulder their responsibility.

However, I am a woman who befriends prostituted women. I feel their pain as they seek to integrate into and maintain a family. It is time for macho men to understand that internet pornography feeds lust, and the God who looked for Adam and Eve seeks you, too. Male perpetrators will probably lose their home, family, status, and self-worth by stealing from the equally vulnerable trapped in a repetitive cycle of destructive behaviour. Why not contact Charles or me and try our discipling journey that might also require the assistance of a psychologist?

Survival and mayhem – why?

In the townships, life went on. Liquor restrictions brought out the worst in some. Raiding liquor stores. Grown women scaling high fences to be first in line for limited alcohol supplies. Making and selling African beer for R35 a litre. Others buy this over food for their families. Youth gangs in Philippi hijacked a truck filled with gas bottles.

Then came a phone call. The simple gift from a friend was like a hug from my God when Debbie called, "I've baked bread. Pick up some fresh from the oven on your way home." All lockdown rules considered, we drove by and through an open car window received warm, buttered, delicious bread, a welcome gift for our family.

We saw police and the army at roadblocks on our major roads. Why were they absent in the townships? Was this meant to protect specific sectors of our city more than others? I wondered about that as we drove.

Animals at peace

By lockdown day 24, the severe curtailment of human movement continued, and our precious earth began to restore its balance. I love seeing pictures of animals at peace. Giraffes along the now quiet N7, snakes crossing the usually busy N7, penguins wading down Simonstown Main Road with no cars in sight, a pride of lions lying relaxed and stretched out in the sun on a car-deserted road in Kruger National Park.

However, nature's balance was restored with birdsong and unexpected pleasures. Six giraffes were grazing next to the R27. I gasped with wonder as they fed in peace, enjoying God's provision for them. However, humankind cowered in fear at an unseen viral demon on the other side of the fence.

Contrast those images with our human condition at that time. Anxiety, fear, frenzy, panic, helplessness. Let us ponder the avaricious greed of those corrupt individuals driving the little-understood pandemic. This unseen and mutating virus brought nations to a standstill[94].

Is there no need to ponder the need for a renewed commitment by Christians to disciple others to address the distancing between the Gospel and those for whom the Saviour died?

A different Easter

On 12 April 2020, Andrea Bocelli performed for the world in an empty cathedral. The pathos of it moved me beyond tears as the music washed over my soul and the cameras moved to empty cities worldwide. The pictures of our abandoned world were as moving to watch as the songs he sang.

Easter was different – surreal. We shared communion with a few friends over the internet as we reflected on our faith in our risen Lord Jesus Christ. Somehow, we did not enjoy the single Easter egg and missed the traditional extended family time – and the pickled fish.

Notwithstanding, my friend Debbie baked bread again. No visits. No tea. Just a distant handover. She also gave me two homegrown sweet potatoes that contributed to the enjoyment of a delicious meal and left some for replanting. Looking at that beautiful sweet potato with its green shoots gave me so much hope for this life in Christ that is real and cannot be buried.

Boxed in - a city of contrasts

The school in the USA where my twelve-year-old granddaughter Halle attended was in lockdown too.

---

94 Romans 5.12.

The children were asked to depict their feelings during quarantine in an art piece. Halle's winning entry was entitled "Boxed In". It captured the feeling brilliantly. I could identify with it immediately. Can you?

The last few days have contrasted strongly with the Easter Message of death and resurrection. The treatment of the homeless, forceful demolition of shacks, civil unruliness and dangerous looting of stores had captured the minds of the broken. However, discipleship remained our focus, and I had a memorable time with one of those ladies that day. I wanted to hug her, but - lockdown rules! She had to read my eyes to see my smile under my mask.

In understanding a child

The contrasts were just as disturbing as we continued with relief efforts and moved with due caution through various communities.

Some of us could lock down safely. Enough food and even luxuries, safe home grounds and a pool for our children to play, a room full of toys, TV games and consoles, E-learning and home-schooling all set up. With access to technology, parents could work from home and run their virtual offices.

However, the coin's flipside revealed different realities for countless other families in townships, informal settlements, and farm labourer communities across our nation – they were excluded. My frustration level was at its peak. How was it even possible that I could buy a milk tart but not purchase wax crayons and colour-in books for children who have nothing to keep them meaningfully stimulated? They had no green grass to play on. Sand, tar, gravel and dirt were their only playing fields as their play mimicked violent adult behaviour.

We desperately needed to give these children an essential activity pack along with our food packs. But the stores would not sell them to me. Not wax crayons. Not colour in - books. It is not considered essential school stationery.

However, I needed an affidavit from the police that I would not sell it. Still, the police could not help me until I approached the station commander. Eventually, we were told to find a Commissioner of Oaths. I only wanted to purchase some wax crayons and colouring books! "Aren't little children also a priority in these crazy times?" I asked. As my temper frayed, I suddenly remembered my father sitting on the steps of our forced removal Bridgetown home. He sat silently gazing at Table Mountain and soliloquised, "Such a beautiful mountain. Such a lot of stupid people."

Troubled days

We moved off to a new township to the north. While driving along the central road bordered by neat houses protected by high walls and fences, we found ourselves in another world.

Then, when crossing a junction, the contrast hit me like a fist in the gut - the landscape changed in a flash – on the same road!

The house we took some food to was simple but clean. A family doing all they could to get an education for their children and come out as overcomers. But uncollected dirt had piled up around the corner. Raw sewage was damming in the roads around them because of blocked street drains. People lived, and children played in that area. Maybe poor communities have an advanced immune system because they and their children survived in conditions our children could not. Corona-19, you may have met your match, I mused.

No, it was not an easy day, and I asked my God, "Can you help us to get this right, please?". The blocked overflowing drains I spoke about earlier had been cleared – the City fathers had responded quickly to our call. But I did not expect it to stay clean and clear for long because the antediluvian infrastructure cannot cope with the influx of people.

The end of a troubled week

We listened to government ministers address the nation and the media. What they said about lockdown rules went over many people's heads. This reminded me of some aspects of televangelism, where preachers don't know their audience. They pump their message with appeals for cash while strutting about in their designer-made clothes, glittering jewellery and Gucci shoes. The townships, informal settlements and farming communities are different. Life has its own rules there. People determine what their survival priorities are. COVID-19 concerns had little chance of competing with hunger, job and financial insecurity.

In some communities, groups of young boys call an UBER vehicle. They then hijack the vehicle and rob drivers of their mobile phones. Opportunities to sell the phone were a street away. Of course, the value of cables and copper on the illegal market brought in necessary cash (and no income tax). The outcomes left the roads in darkness and railways without trains. Do we understand the desperate plight of those who exist well below the breadline? After all, the survival need is a primary component of our evolutionary journey

The lighter moments

We watched a cow leading her calves instinctively halt at a stop sign. We saw a child's face light up, not for an X-Box but for the small box of wax crayons and a colouring-in book.

However, the most hilarious five minutes of prime-time television was watching our President demonstrate how to fit on a face mask - and his response. That laugh took the sting out of all the disturbing images that day.

Social distancing – conundrum or blessing

It is high time that we did away with the social distancing between class and religion and the staying away from communicating with neighbours where we live. The tool to use is inclusive discipleship which will embrace all for whom Christ died.

The gig economy and an iconic reminder of my God

Poor communities on the beautiful West Coast were struggling to feed their families. Cleaners, farm labourers and domestic workers were unpaid during the lockdown.

How can legislation ensure the provision of holiday and sick pay and provide a pension scheme and benefits for full-time contracted workers but not for those in the gig economy[95]? Yet again, those in power positions exploit workers. Arguably, all workers – whether employed or from the gig economy should be paid the same and receive a proportion of the benefits against the time worked ... labourers are worthy of their hire[96].

Anomalies

We saw police and the army at roadblocks on our major roads. Why were they absent in the township?

Teaching children how to wash their hands was fun in one area where they had shared taps. However, how were they expected to keep to this routine when walking two kilometres to collect water from another site?

Trouble escalates

Crime is endemic across Cape Town, and its incredible beauty contrasts with extreme violence and lawlessness. We have witnessed and experienced that first-hand. Recent news reports list Cape Town as the most violent City in Africa and the eighth most violent in the world. Yet we are the most highly churched city. Twenty-eight years into our democracy, our townships on the Cape Flats are the most dangerous areas. Post-Apartheid South Africa still shudders from the fallout of the repressive laws described in earlier chapters.

---

[95] A gig economy is one where companies hire independent contractors and freelancers instead of taking on full-time workers. In a gig economy, temporary positions are common, but full-time permanent ones are not. The gig economy is becoming an increasingly common feature in most countries across the world today (https://marketbusinessnews.com/financial-glossary/gig-economy-definition-meaning/).
[96] 1 Timothy 5.18.

We saw criminality in different forms, played out in front of us repeatedly. Lockdown seemed to accentuate our awareness of it. Ahead of us, another UBER was highjacked. To steal the cell phone and use the car in another violent robbery. Community justice threatened to play itself out in the same area as a young boy darted across the road to get in on the action. Police arrived in time. Next, we were just a few hours too late, it seemed. A busted safe was lying on the field we parked on, where two weeks previously, a truck transporting gas tanks was highjacked and looted.

I wondered how much money was in the safe, Or was it busted for a firearm? Did anyone see this being dumped there? Surely someone did. However, they will remain silent because the gangster bosses pay their rent and electricity and give them food and liquor on credit. Indeed, Pavlov and his eye on stimuli and conditioning still make sense.

Why?

An ineffective church has largely forgotten its mandate. Are we, as the church of Jesus, celebrating the wrong things. At the same time, we lose the next generation, and our children become more desensitised to the violence around them. Perhaps we should throw our church clocks on the table, start again by reading the instruction manual, and follow Jesus' unambiguous instructions.

Labels that create barriers

I dislike the modern and random use of the term "the poor." Debatably, it comes with elitist perceptions, thoughtless intolerance and divisive judgement. I hate taking pictures of people receiving gifts to prove to a donor that we have actually given them to "the poor and needy." I am cautious about that. Can you imagine what it must do a father's pride and dignity when we take pictures of his wife and children gratefully receiving the gifts? I always wonder about that. And the barrier it can create as we seek to disciple a father to transform his family.

Lockdown accentuated this anomaly of "them and us". How much longer can we live in a city and a country with such stark contrasts when twenty minutes in either direction, socioeconomic disparities exist? It seems like a recipe for disaster and turns back the pages of history to the French Revolution that shook France between 1787 and 1799 and reached its first peak in 1789. Will South Africa's next war purge the arrogance of discriminatory class privilege – a resurrection of the thoughts of Karl Marx and further pogroms of hate?

> Then the king will say to those at his right hand, 'Come, you that are blessed by my Father, inherit the kingdom prepared for you from the foundation of the world; for I was hungry, and you gave me food, I was thirsty, and you gave me something to drink, I was a stranger, and you welcomed me, I was naked, and you gave me clothing, I was sick, and you took care of me, I was in prison, and you visited me[97].

Housing crises

We were driving out of a township on the West Coast when we were dumbstruck at the sight of about fifty brand-new houses and a youth centre deliberately and criminally vandalised -

---
97 Matthew 25. 34-36.

destroyed. Damaged so severely that no one has been able to take occupancy since we saw it for the first time a year ago! Nothing had changed. I could not understand this. People told us that the fifty-plus houses were destroyed by those unhappy with the allocation of the would-have-been-homes. Was this carnage a reaction against the corruption where political pawns get bribed to enable families to bypass the housing waiting list? Is it the enactment of the psychology of being the underdog?

Is this the result of politicising the housing crisis?

Is it fear of retaliation that allows one to see and hear the destruction and do nothing? Or is it just not my business? I recall the story of the Good Samaritan[98]. I note those who crossed by on the other side of the road. Ah, the "outsider" came to help, and that assistance had a total financial cost attached in advance.

Corruption runs rampant across all government sectors, businesses and society, and even some bodies representing the church. On the other hand, Charles feels strongly that corruption is too often given a black face. White corrupters have the money, education, work environment and connections to hide their deeds and invest in global markets. Allegedly, they corrupted persons across the colour lines who aspired after wealth and the trappings of money. I recall the saying, if someone says, "It's not the money, it's the principle," then you must ask them to define what they mean by "principle".

---

98 John 4. 5-43.

Kintsugi

I love this Japanese art method. The skilled repairing of broken ceramic objects by joining each piece into a new whole, with gold, silver, or platinum, affirms a historical and unique entity.

I have rejoiced repeatedly in seeing that happen in people's lives. So when I feel the despair of broken life fragments in the people we meet, I remember Kintsugi art and the work of Jesus, whose message[99] every discipling emissary shares:

> The Spirit of the Lord God is upon me,
> Because the Lord has anointed me
> To bring good news to the afflicted;
> He has sent me to bind up the broken-hearted,
> To proclaim liberty to captives
> And freedom to prisoners.

The core focus of discipling others is to introduce individuals to the process used by the divine potter, best described by Jeremiah[100]. The illustration of the potter and the wheel aptly outlines the process of what theology cites as sanctification. Crucially, this is a process that makes allowances for the imperfect to grow into maturity.

I recall walking just a little behind some precious young women beginning to take their baby steps out of prostitution towards Jesus ... life ... hope ... and a future. Other ministry partners devote their lives to this cause. I continue to learn as they disciple me in my ministry.

---

99 Isaiah 61.1.
100 Jeremiah 18.

Homelessness and discipleship

We spent many nights with homeless adults in different parts of our city. Every race, skin colour, culture, and faith or lack of a spiritual source. Some have little or no education, while others come from a professional niche. Of course, there are reasons why an individual resorts to street living, but nevertheless, each cries out for change. Discipleship must expand further into the highways and byways of society.

In the eye of the storm and discipleship

A storm was brewing over Cape Town, and lightning illuminated the sky while the thunder disturbed me. Then, I heard the rapid rounds of gunfire and the sound of bullets in crossfire in a contained space. We stopped the car, and a deathly pall hung over Hanover Park. Lockdown regulations were not high on the community agenda here. Then all hell broke loose. War. Unending gun war. Long protracted peals of repetitive fire.

I was a community health nurse in this same community decades ago. So I had dodged bullets before, but the sounds had died in my head. The fifty litres of hot soup had to wait while we took cover in the house of friends who would share the soup with their neighbours. Who cares about social distancing when you must dodge bullets? We took shelter in the confined space of the little house in the middle of a gang war zone.

A mother and grandmother's tearful, anxious sobs responded to the news that a young baby would have to wait for his mother to return home. We heard that one man had been killed by a bullet through his head. The ambulance had to wait for the police escort to a hospital in another township. The local hospital closes at 1900 because of the constant gang violence.

However, our presence reassured the family, who had received assurance that all their grandchildren were safe. I pondered whether raising an emotionally healthy child from birth to adulthood in this environment was possible. How do you teach a child to dream bold dreams for their lives in a violent environment like this? How do you teach the values of respect, care and Ubuntu (I am because you are) in this environment that does not regard life as precious?

Youth Day and the Gospel

South Africa commemorates the day in 1976 when over 500 young people were ambushed and killed by security police in Soweto. One of the issues motivating the unrest was forcing black students to learn Afrikaans.

In the 21st century, young people are still killed in post-Apartheid South Africa today – for different reasons. Violence, while centuries old, is a systemic part of much of South Africa's social structure. It is a curse that must be broken in the spiritual realm, and Christian discipleship can address the spiritual issues. Imagine the impact if the problems of social and Biblical justice were handled with the same political will and fervour as with the COVID-19 pandemic.

A day of extremes

Before midday Charles and I had held two pairs of hands in ours. One young man as he lay dying. He had come to faith in Christ a few weeks previously. Simply. Quietly. To be homeless and dying alone is heartbreaking. We had intense conversations about life, mistakes, regrets, forgiveness, and freedom in Christ. We rejoice in where he is today in Heaven, where he is understood and accepted. He will never be homeless, rejected, or misunderstood again.

Then a short while later, we sat with our friend, an undocumented prostituted woman from another African country. Over breakfast, once a week, I was doing Life Plan discussions with her, helping her to see the God clues in her tragic story. Clues about her identity and her gifting. And her purpose. That Wednesday morning, without prompting, she asked us to help her accept Christ as her Saviour. What a morning that was. From profound sadness to breath-taking delight. All in the morning. She decided that morning that she was done with prostitution and would leave for home. She set a date. We spoke about how she would survive. With the help of a fellow disciple-maker in our extended network, we set up a small business that she could run from home. She texted me on the long-distance bus home, "I trust you, and I trust your God".

"Oh my God, only you can make this happen," was often my cry.

The smell of broccoli

Then to lighten my mood, my God stepped in. Those who know Charles will know he hates certain vegetables, like pumpkin, cabbage, cauliflower and broccoli. He cannot even tolerate the smell. It makes him sick. So, my God decided to rain down broccoli on us! Sixty heads of the freshest broccoli!

Charles had to collect it using a small car surrounded by the suffocating broccoli smell. Well, how to maximise this supply of broccoli? "I know, I'll make broccoli and cheese soup! You'll have to help me chop all this up!" Charles recoiled but got stuck in. It seemed we would never stop chopping.

Over the next two days, we served over 200 cups of hot broccoli and cheese soup. The people on the streets loved it, but I could not get Charles to taste it.

Broken pieces

I learn so much from people recovering from brokenness. One woman who experienced healing from extreme brokenness said something I will never forget. She said, "If you give a broken person broken clothes, you make them more broken." She hit the nail right on the head for me. As I was writing this story, I recall a colleague telling me of the time when a donation had arrived. Upon opening it, a box of used tea bags was amongst some torn and dirty second-hand clothing. Yes, broken pieces that probably soothed a donor's conscience – but … Why?

Word pictures

The devil has always tried to disrupt our lives and ministry.

During one severe winter, a heavily pregnant woman sleeping on a thin folded blanket on an icy pavement in the pelting rain needed help. Our friend Lorenzo helped us find immediate safe accommodation for her. Her healthy baby girl was born by Caesarean Section two weeks later.

I was subsequently threatened and sworn at – in the most vulgar way – by the man who had fathered this child. He threatened to get his gang friends to kill Charles. I wondered about his childhood and the type of father he had. I mused over his family life. Did he know the difference between being a dad and fathering a child? The baby is safe in foster care, supported by the maternal grandmother and older siblings.

Yes, the lives of so many are fragmented and need the potter's hand to reshape them. Discipleship makes it possible for broken chords to vibrate once more. The fields are ready for harvesting. I recall the words of a friend's sermon many years ago when he said, "do not ask the Lord for a vision – just open your eyes and get off your chair and go ..." to the neighbours next door and across the street.

Liquor restrictions go – along with dignity

The liquor outlets opened, and Voortrekker Road was a mass of people waiting for the store's gates to open. However, the fences surrounding the building had served as ladders for many to jump the queue. Security guards were powerless to intervene. I watched in amazement as women climbed the gates, clutching their skirts and handbags. It was a disturbing sight.

I wondered why I felt so disturbed. After all, I had seen the bare face and harshness of poverty. I had faced the damaging effects of alcoholism on families and on children. Yet the women scaling the fence were not as poor as others. Questions without ready answers – that is the mayhem environment.

The raw face of poverty

I was reading Salman Rushdie's graphically written book, "The Ground Beneath Her Feet", where he focuses on the sometimes-irretrievable brokenness in our world and our humanness. His words reminded me of South Africa's national brokenness. While we pick up the pieces in our broken city,

Humpty Dumpty totters on the wall. Can we ever put the pieces together again – the legacy of some four centuries of brutalising discrimination and the harsh separation of the land from the First People? Then my thoughts turn to the disciples who trudged the highways and byways of Roman injustice – the onus is on us to follow in their footsteps and engage in discipleship.

In the ghetto

I found myself easily angered by things happening around me. It was just past midnight. And I was 6 days short of being 70 years old. I should have been asleep. That evening, while driving home from transporting goods to a family whose home and livelihood had been destroyed by fire, I turned on the car radio to hear Elvis Presley sing, "In the ghetto".

The song's words challenged me. Charles and I committed to walk in step with God into our broken city, see lives transformed by the Gospel of Jesus, and journey with them as they hold the hand of a friend.

Conclusion

My story has provided snippets of the real South Africa from one of the millions who grew up in a country where foreigners had paid scant respect for the culture of the First People. The outcomes of the developing popularity of what was ironically named THE CAPE OF GOOD HOPE by foreigners who saw its value to accelerate trade. However, those who stayed were from different cultures and failed to find agreement on core issues, so one group departed from the environs of Cape Town. Eventually, people of foreign extraction governed South Africa. At the same time, those born there were excluded from the right to franchise. A warped interpretation of the Bible led to the introduction of Apartheid.

The narrative then meandered through the political, economic and social horrors caused by the Apartheid tsunami. I attempted to introduce the Bible-endorsed practice of discipleship to correct traditions that created Churchianity. However, there is hope for South Africa when church members engage in discipleship.

So, Charles and I have entered through broken gates to sit with shattered people and have often suffered hurt. We have come face to face with the worst that this sprawling city has to offer. The extraordinary challenges of the past few years have impacted us as a family. I often gaze at our majestic Table Mountain and reflect on how the Apartheid tsunami began to gain momentum. I return to that life-changing night when the Lord swept me into his arms and think of my God's grace, mercy and love.

I have learned that our struggles and vulnerabilities as a family cannot be hidden from the people we are discipling. They have seen us relate to my God in our most joyful times, and they have seen us connect to our God in our deepest despair. They have noticed that we make mistakes, fail, and have times of doubt and fear. But they have watched us negotiate those killer tsunamis that cast us on our Rock Jesus. That is what disciple-making is about, and as Zephaniah reminds us[101], the people of God have a tremendous responsibility on their hands.

---

[101] Zephaniah Chapter 3.

As I ended this narrative, I recalled the words that set my life in motion:

> For we are God's handiwork, created in Christ Jesus to do good works, which God prepared in advance for us to do.

May I ask for your prayers as Charles and I – as a husband-and-wife team - continue to disciple others and faithfully complete the responsibilities set out for our attention? Would you also pray for those whose names feature in this book – the heroes?

Let us, one and all, arise and disciple others – South Africa's doldrums experience must end.

www.ingramcontent.com/pod-product-compliance
Lightning Source LLC
Chambersburg PA
CBHW070644160426
43194CB00009B/1577